AF378981

Regi Weile
Axiom Maxiom Drawing Center
Asheville, NC
email: regiweile@axiom-maxiomdrawingcenter.com
Book and Cover design by Laura Ladendorf
Printing by IngramSpark Publishing
Distribution online via Amazon.com and
IngramSpark Publishing

Cover drawing by Maria Epes

Axiom Maxiom Drawing Center   Volumes 1-14 2020-2021

regi weile

A Conference of Birds
in the time of COVID

TABLE OF CONTENTS

PREFACE
The Post at Our Table
Startled by the bellowing Silence, we attested our delivery into quarantine; into the cinctured protection of barricading sticks-and-mortar. It was like a pre-vagitus Silence, depriving us the comforting 'Voice' that soothes germination.

Covid,

A pulse like, circumfluent Chant resonated through the Silence.

warning

COVID, Covid, COVID, covid ,covid … 'COVID' …

of raging contagion.

Covid, Covid, Covid…covid…c o v i d… c…o…v…i…d

'Covid' at first was a term of etymological uncertainty. Dictionaries and even reliable search engines responded to queries drawing the familiar conclusion of 'no results found'. Both magical and quasi-scientific offerings attempted explanation for its sudden appearance by issuing research of phantasmagorical hypothesis.

Was It … Plague? Science-fiction? multi-National threat? Prank? Plague? Global hallucination? Political Propaganda? Pandemic? 'Covid' warned of potential mortal consequences which gave rise to drastic steps towards self-imposed quarantine. The ramifications of a 'quarantine' were known to be as dire as the threatened illness itself. Isolation of this sort, could obliterate, hobble, communicative cultural literary in its vital capacity. As a recurrent challenge in historical recounting, it was known to have had the potential to bring down entire civilizations.

We watched the clock of knowledge … surveying its maturation from primitive storytelling to an effectual development of our schooled civilization. Revealed in its upswing, the versatile 'Voices' tendency extended conversant vocabularies of Hand, Eye, Ear, and spirit-de-corps of mental imagery. It's downswing, however, revealed an apparent muting of the 'Voices' of conversant thought. A muted 'Voice', reduced in scale to soliloquy, [monologue] condemning one to bouts of shadow-boxing within the corner crevices of one's secluded Mind.

For most of us, celestial intervention and plagues were a great attribute of sunday school education. Plagues, as taught, had always been followed by expeditious convalescent-treks. They were testimony to the testing of discipline, in decade long duration, through hostile landscapes or politics. They were meant to end well. Protection and survival were imagined as gifted from the sun, with a cloud-like umbrella by day and with a fiery light by night. Time ran counter-clockwise always returning a new day and never retracting progress. Past-time easily forgotten, always eclipsed by New-time.

Noah was the first to teach us about quarantine … and then about Bird-flight. Noah had been coerced into inhabiting an Ark-of-Quarantine. For 360 days he was separated from all errant life forms. He witnessed a scourge of dissolution, in which all matter of life was dissolved into nothingness by floods of water from above and below. Protected, he floated on the abysmal sea in quarantine. Desperately wishing to receive some desirable information from the unseen celestial power responsible for his dilemma, Noah sent a Bird forth as his Ambassador. And she, as the first carrier pigeon, brought back genuine signs that were useful and diligently enlisted.

Carrier Pigeons

Myth and History, both fictional creations, present ample evidence of exemplary resolutions for communication across measurable distances of deserts, oceans, prairies; and immeasurable distances longitudinal, latitudinal, sub-terrain, mythic. Charting the mysteries of plagues, floods, tempests, and wars, however, were never assuredly resolvable.

It became a priority of enigmatic proportion for us when the sudden distancing by quarantine threatened the curtailment of in-person communication of conversant thought. Could it be possible to parrot Noah's resourceful use of Birds to maintain communication during quarantine by resorting to supernal communication in the flight of Ambassadorial pigeons?

Efforts to replicate the remedy of 'Ambassadorial Flight' were contemplated and then undertaken in our Studio. The prime figure for Ambassadorial service was to be the Carrier Pigeon. Each Participant chose a Bird purposed for this responsibility. Drawings of Birds and their mask-like replications arrived in our studio by postal carrier or drop-box delivery. Images of herons, doves, crows, owls and falcons hovered over the studio, peering out of an eternal timelessness.

The Post of the Carrier Pigeon, a branch of service available to the historic pioneering settlers, had served in its time, to knit together discourse allowing the evolution of an adhesively bound Community. It was now to be re-purposed, reassessed in replication, to insure maintenance of our possible Global Community challenged in quarantine. It was further considered in its role to insure a sturdy basis for a hopeful trek of future convalescence. Correspondence by mail or postal carrier opened options for the continuance of civilized dialogic writing, drawing, painting, socialization and music. We set to work, at Axiom Maxiom, exploring and analyzing characteristics of the selected Birds to serve as Ambassadors capable of directing flow of communication … to engender a newly revived

Post at our Table

and new City in the Air!

regi weile

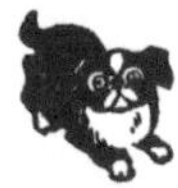

AS THIS, SO THAT
learning to listen, to see, and to focus

Noah's Birds

When the flood began to subside Noah sent out three BIRDS to confirm the earth's habitability.

He first sent out the Raven. The Raven flew about in circles, believing that it was driven out because of his bad behavior. It did not trust Noah, having been forced to leave its mate aboard the Ark. It did not agree to this 'mission' and circled about to then return to the Ark.

Noah then sent out the Swallow. The swallow was known for its swiftness of flight and the fact that it could catch its insect food on the wing thereby eliminating the need for stopovers. It had the capacity to fly, even though in circles, up to 600 miles per day. Its flight was horizontal and dependent in direction upon the food availed in its passage. It completed its 'mission' but found no dry land in any direction and so returned to the Ark. The Swallow suggested to Noah that a Pigeon or Dove might be more

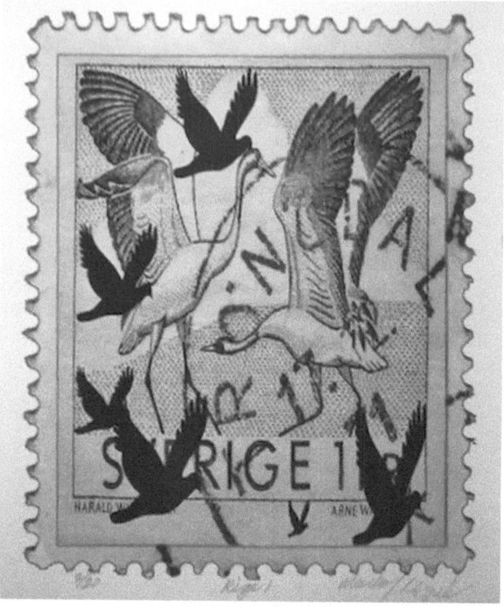

Postal Correspondence

Correspondence-courses were the earliest form of distance-education. Their intent was communication as an intermingling of language giving voice to ink on paper with gestural annotations configured to transmit thought in space. These correspondences were by mandate, enveloped in mysterious foldings and impressed with waxed or stamped shields for invulnerable transport.

Employed in distance-education, they promoted a familial form of interaction. With the lack of accessibility, having to reach long distances across the prairie lands of America for discourse, the need to bridge remoteness was a great challenge. Satisfaction was found, by default, successful, as they could reach heights of up to 6,000 feet and travel 92.5 mph. Perhaps, the Swallow thought, the dry land that Noah sought was above the horizon, vertically and not parallel to it.

Noah then sent out the Dove, from the carrier pigeon family. Its flight was not only more suited to the 'mission' but could be augmented by the Doves ability to see in color and recognize itself in reflective surfaces. In addition it had the ability to communicate and understand human intelligence in the language of…taking orders. The Dove departed on its 'mission' never to return to the Ark…nor did it send any correspondence related to its distant whereabouts. This was thought to have been an indication that the Swallow had been correct in suggesting the path of search as being above the horizon and infinitely outward and upward in scale and direction. Noah declared the 'mission' complete and disembarked upon the heights of Mt. Ararat.

regi weile

with those in close proximity. An assignment received at home by Post, could be shared in its revelations at the family table. Be that as it may, a reply post-haste in exchange was implied in its receipt.

Receipt of a Postal assignment, in promise of an educational exchange, brought a contagious excitement on the part of the teacher/educator that inspired the learner to move forward in discovery.

And what diversion of spirit there could be in restoring that excitement for today's participants. To once again anticipate the receipt of a postal envelope containing a startling assignment, a question … or even on some occasions … an answer. An assignment addressed to everyone standing together at the foot of our mountains, on our grassland, under our cabin threshold or seated at our table. An assignment anticipated for renewed discourse.

The post-at-the-table gave voice to co-participants; the everyone-the-educator, addressing the everyone-the-learner. The everyone-the-educator became the voice of the guide, helper and…sometimes mentor. The ensuing Dialogues at table, extended from family, to neighbor, to congregation and promised to become the precursor of the new American classroom. With a storm of newly articulated discussions, readings, music, writings and performances, the Arts and Sciences could surge in advancement.

As the inhabitants of our era of the electronic usurpation of communication by technology, we bear witness to the appropriation of our hand and voice in being morphed by an industry of soulless anonymity. Its imposition, its

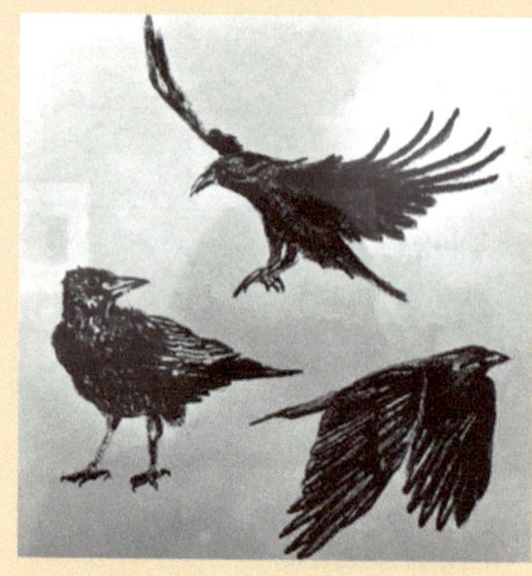

intervention, replaced, if not annihilated the equitable usefulness of the voice in literate and postal exchange. The personal soliloquy of letter writing was abandoned in its purposeful fulfillment of cultural and developmental aspiration. Our Democratized exchanges were despoiled and demoralized … much as a 'plundered city bared to the wind'.

Safety considerations in our time of Covid, removed the American classroom from consideration. Its replacement by Virtual Learning moved the teacher and learner into a vacuous electronic world of isolation.

We proposed to abandon the computerized-classroom, restore learning to the table of the American home and return to a correspondence-instruction that could afford the socialization lacking in our current alternatives.

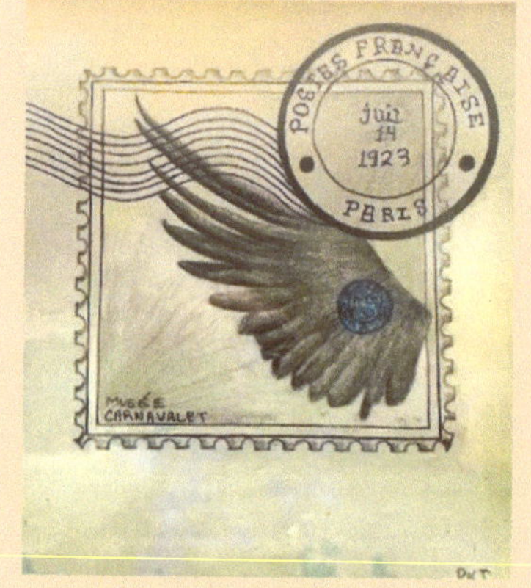

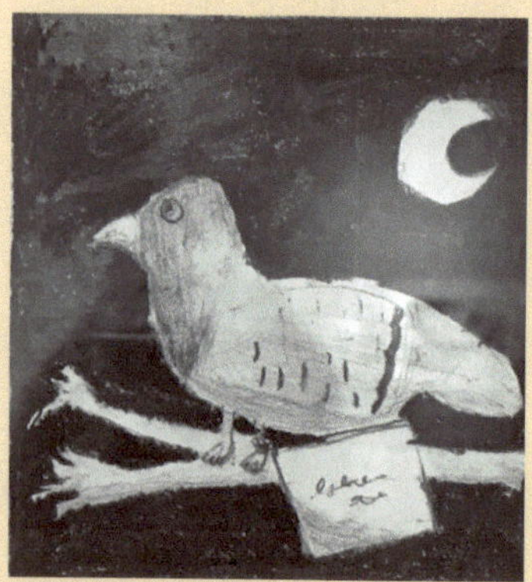

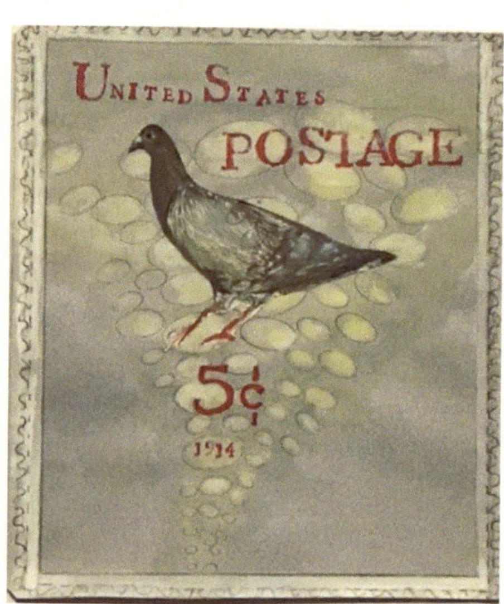

There can be a return to the contagious excitement on the part of the teacher/educator that inspires the student/learner to move forward in discovery.

AND

There can be a return to the contagious excitement on the part of the student/learner that inspires the teacher/educator to move forward in discovery.

And what diversity there could be in restoring that excitement for all participants; to restore the excitement of awaiting, in anticipation, the receipt of a postal envelope containing a startling assignment, a question … or even on some occasions … an answer. An envelope addressed to everyone standing together at the foot of our mountains, or seated at our tables. An assignment anticipating the renewal of the inclination to see, to listen and to focus personally in an exchange.

End of Episode One

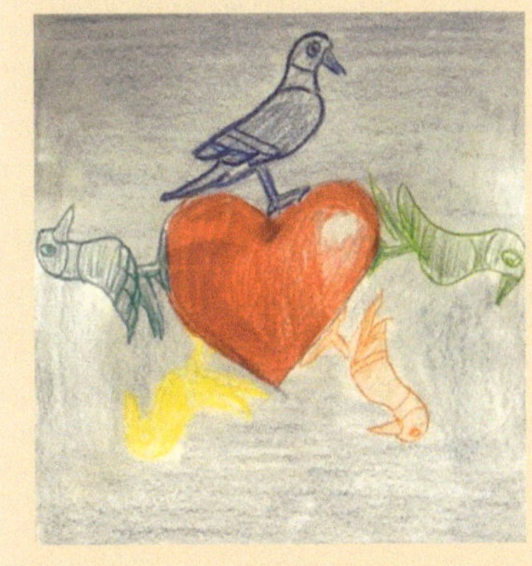

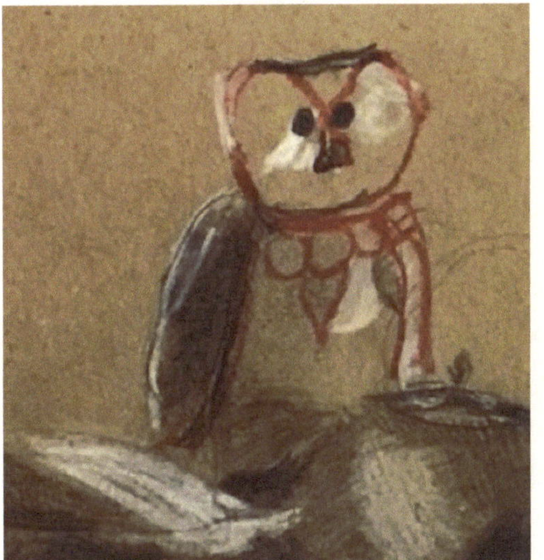

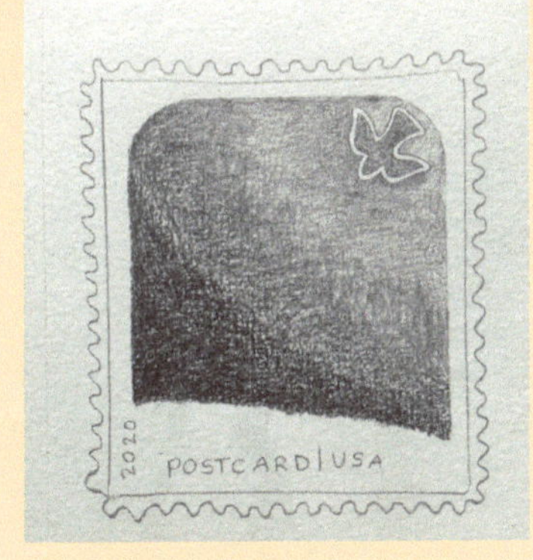

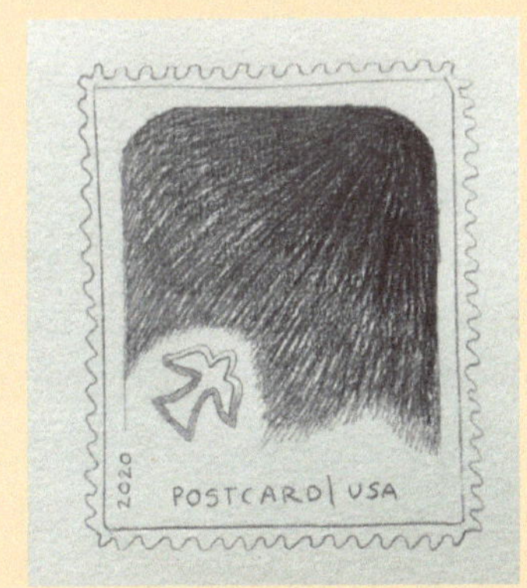

Assignment One:
BIRD STAMPS

Choose a Bird and transform its image into a commemorative STAMP. Add a note as to its dedicatory significance in history and the future.

in the air

The air is the appropriate abode for the winged race, its element by nature is Light. It is the proper home for these creatures who are also light by reason of being feathered. They are creatures whose nature it is to traverse the air and roam through the aether. Bird flight is upward in height, conducting its mind towards infinite and heavenly aspirations of thought, barely ever descending a foot onto earth.

a' Philo

The air also serves as the appropriate abode for the human mind, its element, by nature, being Light. It is the proper home for those who are by reason imaginative. Their minds traverse the air allowing them to roam through the aether and easily bring back genuine pleasure, wisdom and that which is fruitful. Like an Ambassador, the mind brings back what is useful and can be diligently expounded upon if carefully enlisted.

Even though the human is bound gravitationally to the material earth, their true abode is in the hovering element above … gracing the earths surface only for mundane service, assured that the memory of supernal space accompanies them there in their efficacy.

Assignment Two:
the CONVEX and CONCAVE VISION
Draw Light from a circumferential perimeter inward and from a central point outward.

In order to understand the flight of the Bird, understanding the rhythmic 'convex and concave' motion of the wings is essential.

The Universe was made as a sphere, even and smooth, perfect, alone and sufficient to itself. It's revolutions, caused the substances of air to trigger a great fire of light with which to make its existence visible. Imitating the shape of this spherical Universe, two smaller globe-shaped rotating-spheres were set within its orbit. One contained a molten fire at its center and the other, a smaller globe, held at its center … a soul of concavity. This smaller sphere was gifted with 7 apertures with which to discern the senses.

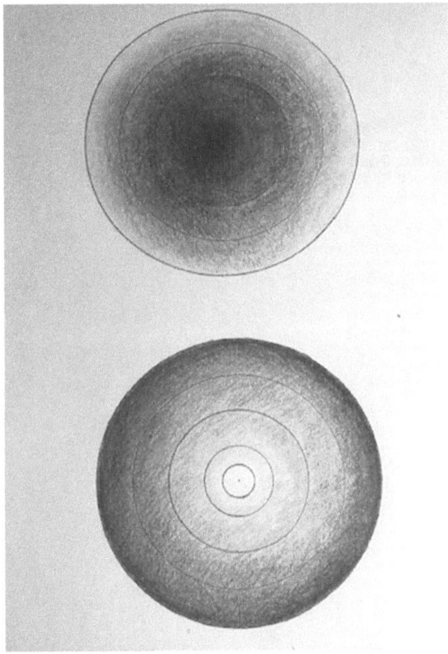

CIRCLE ONE: The fiery light lit the earth externally from its furthest circumferential ring. Draw the progressive absence of light as the rings move inward away from light and towards the amorphous darkness at its center. The Light of the Universe, try as it may, cannot completely penetrate the material density of the earth's circumference causing suggestions of concavity. Draw the light to dark gradations of the circles with black pencil on white paper. [5B to 9B pencils]

CIRCLE TWO: The fiery global sphere, with the center of molten fire, warmed the earth's circle from within, with gradations of light moving towards the darkness of its circumferential ring. Lit in this manner the earth circumference caused the apparency of convexity. This as a reversal of the Drawing above to be Drawn in black pencil on white paper. [2B to 5B pencils]

WHITE CIRCLES ON BLACK PAPER: repeat the above exercise on the Templates printed on black paper with white pencil.

Submit your **BIRD STAMP** and **CIRCLE DRAWINGS** at our Axiom-Maxiom DropBox or by Snail Mail to 5 Rollingwood Road, Asheville N.C. 28805.

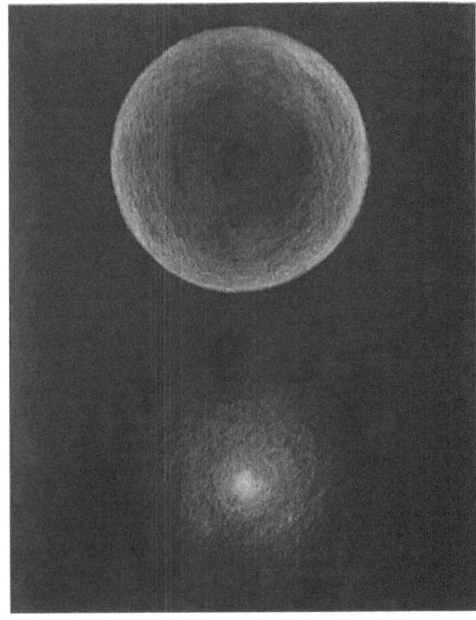

AS THIS, SO THAT

learning to listen, to see, and to focus

Birds

Ralph Waldo Emerson

Darlings of children and of bard,

Perfect kinds by vice unmarred,

All of worth and beauty set

Gems in Natures cabinet;

These the fables she esteems

Reality most like to dreams.

Welcome back, you little nations,

Far-travelled in the south plantations;

Bring your music and rhythmic flight,

Your colors for our eyes' delight:

Freely nestle in our roof,

Weave your chamber weatherproof;

And your enchanting manners bring

And your autumnal gathering.

Exchange in conclave general

Greetings kind to each and all,

Conscious each of duty done

And unstained as the sun.

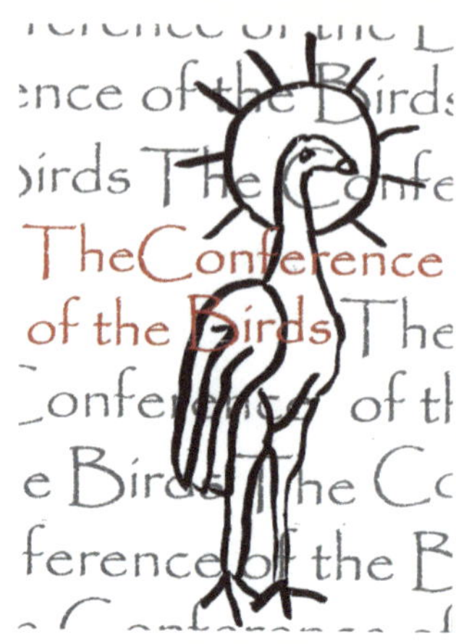

Conference of Birds

… a twice told story…in 414 BC.

Two Athenians, known as Persuader and Hope, fed up with politics and law-courts fled their City and went in search for Tereus the Hoopoe. They believed he might be of help to them in finding a better life somewhere else.

"If you don't know where you are going, any road will take you there"

L.Carroll

Tereus, was found and was sympathetic to their plight. During their interview with him Persuader came up with a magnificent idea: to found a city in the clouds. He had realized that if birds just stop flying around and instead use their time to build a City and empire in the heavens, they might become masters of the Universe. They would thus be able to rule the humans from above — and, by intercepting sacrifices to the gods

— starve the problematic Olympian gods into submission.

With the Hoopoes endorsement, Persuasion concocted a story for the Bird Council that proved they had once been the rulers of the Universe. He managed to convince them that they deserved to rule the Universe again. The idea of a new city was there-to-fore advanced and designated as the municipality of CLOUD-QUILLE, home to all Bird-citizens with the right of return.

Since there is no rose without a thorn…CQ naturally became an annoyance in the eyes of both the humans and their gods. Quite soon incursions into CQ planning by four intruders were detected by the Birds; a feather beater, a poet, an informer and Goddess Iris. The nature and objective of their intrusion is still under investigation.

The Bird Council is currently meeting in a forest, just outside the region of the Hoopoe's nest. Persuasion and Hope are wandering in a wild desolate region nearby searching for the Birds. Each of them has a bird in hand. Hope has a Jay and Persuasion a Crow. These served as guides for them as assigned by the bird-seller.

The Jay and the Crow exhibited their true worth by directing them directly to an Olympian Rock. Hope knocked on the Rock and attracted the attention of **FOOTBIRD*** a majestic servant of the Hoopoe.

Bidden by his servant, the Hoopoe gushed forth from the rock. In his immediacy he appeared to have many prescient intimations as to the possible whereabouts of the place sought.

"Are you looking for a city greater than Athens?" he queried.

"No," replied Hope, "not greater, but one more pleasant to live in."

A number of places were suggested by Hoopoe "a city of delights by the sea, or a city of hanging gardens with cooling pools?" None of those suggested were found suitable.

Interrupting Hope and Hoopoe, Persuasion was struck with another great idea. It was an obvious solution he proclaimed. Their habitat should be situated between the humans and the gods. That is, between the below and the above. "Air," he reasoned "is between the earth below and heaven above. Many have even believed that the air actually holds the heavens in place above the earth."

**footnote one. [FOOTBIRD: I do recall, in my early scientific studies, a footrock. It was a specimen collected for my research … a rock shaped like a foot…or at least the lower part of the foot. Not being familiar with a Footbird but well aquainted with the footrock I recognized the Footbird immediately by genetic impaction. Footbird instructed the wanderers to knock on the Olympian rock [a footrock] in the same manner Moses knocked on a rock as part of a different metaphor].*

Persuasion continued, "every Nation has the right to exact payment of tribute for passage or refusal of foreigners passage through its domain. If travel through Delphi is requested, a leave of passage is needed to be granted exacting tribute; the alternative being a refusal of passage outright. Now, if humankind wishes to send its savory aroma of sacrifice upward to the heavens, the aroma must rise through the air from below and pass through 'your domain' to reach the intended recipient above."

In simple terms, he reiterated, "When men sacrifice or offer prayers to the gods above … you can exercise the right of your city/nation to dis-allow the smoke of the sacrifice to pass through the air of your territory. Not permit the sweet aroma of sacrifice or words of prayer to pass through and reach the above unless tribute is paid to your city." The Hoopoe was enchanted with the plan and believed the scheme to be the best ever conceived … comparable only the toll-roads of memory. In acknowledgement of this creative statute he called together all his Bird-friends.

Here we must introduce the Bird-friends who gathered in an excited chorus of chirps, chits, screeches and cackles. These were Birds of the following varieties: Dove, Falcon, Peacock, Pigeon, Swallow, Owl, Heron, Sparrow, Partridge, Parrot, Nightingale, Cuckoo, and a Duck. They screeched an anthem of patriotic zeal for their City which filled the air with feathered conviction.

For their triumph in resolving this challenge, Persuasion and Hope, were escorted by Hoopoe to a clearing behind the rock and transformed into…Birds. They took an oath to follow and support the Birds pursuit in establishing their new city.

Your AxiomMaxiom Bird will be conscripted into this communal commitment of breeds conjoined in establishing the city CQ.

Additional information was required for this decree of conscription. Let it be known that a Human Council of Athenians, Priests and Gods, in response, convened to stand resistant to the actualization of Persuasion and Hope's vision of CQ. These were Humans representative of the following varieties: King, dervish, hermit, traveler, beggar, saint, thieve, astrologer, walking birds, and chamberlains. Their challenging effrontery will rival those characterized in Lewis Carroll's 'Walking-Stick of Destiny'. We end our prolegomena here with Carroll's familiar "Adieu for the present, my dear friends, you shall hear from me again. "

End of Episode Two

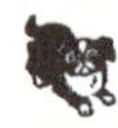

Assignment Three:

In what tree or bower will your bird find a home? Search your property… find a suitable habitable temporary place. Draw its nest as a winter-home until CQ is ready for seasonal migration.

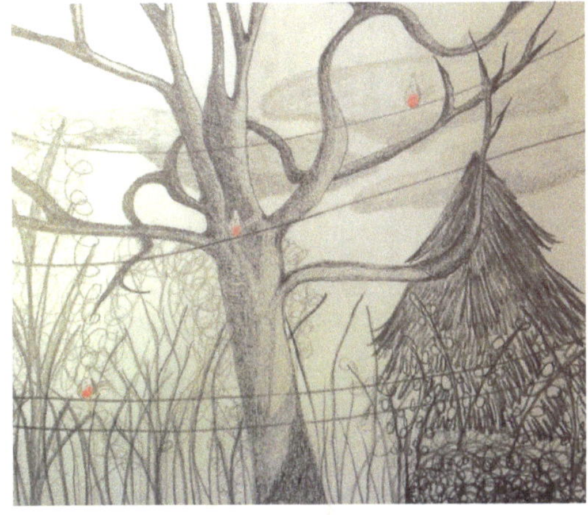

Assignment Four:

Choose a BIRD from Folklore, Mythology, Nursery Rhyme, Fable, or Aristophanes BIRDS.

Draw the BIRD in black and white. Write a brief description of its utility and symbolic identity in establishing its significance … for you.

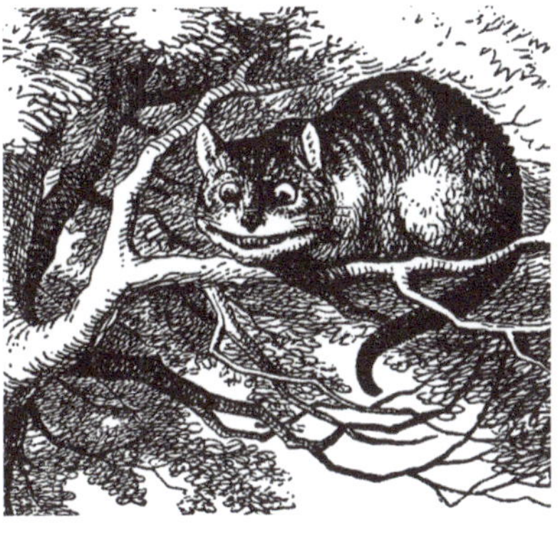

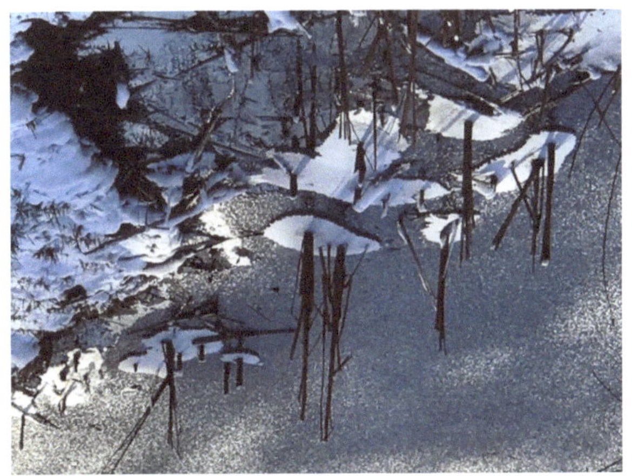

AS THIS, SO THAT

learning to listen, and to see

Birds 328

Emily Dickinson

A Bird came down the
    Walk-

He did not know I saw -
He bit an Angelworm in
    halves

And ate the fellow raw,

And then he drank a Dew
From a convenient Grass -

And then hopped sidewise
    to the Wall

To let a Beetle pass -

He glanced with rapid eyes

That hurried all around -

They looked like frightened
    Beads, I thought -

He stirred his Velvet Head

Like one in danger,
    Cautious,

I offered him a Crumb

And he unrolled his
    feathers

And rowed him softer home

Than Oars divide the
    Ocean,
Too silver for a seam -

Or Butterflies, off Banks of
    Noon

Leap, plashless as they
    swam.

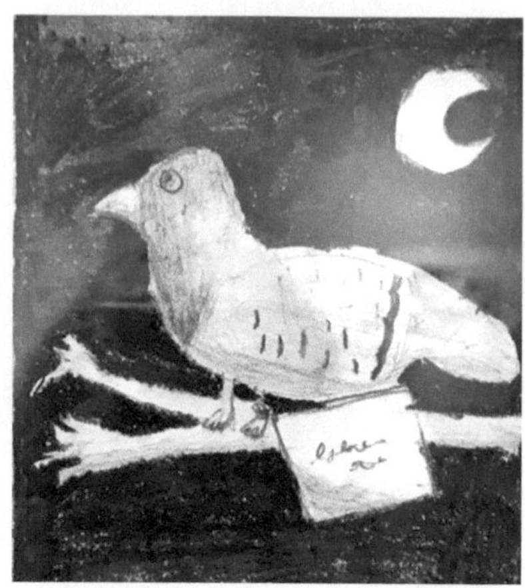

Conference of Birds

Hope was heard to proclaim to no one in particular, "I will measure the air geo-metrically for you, and measure it out in proportion to the earth". This was thought passible as the air is, in form very much like a cosmic house. …a heavenly bowl, a dome or cosmic egg. It was recalled that historically the Athenians erroneously measured it with a straight stick and there-by its circular form became squared.

"The air", Hope continued, " was formed concave, much as a dome-vaulting heaven. Nizami taught us that the inside of the dome reflected the brilliance of the sun, while the outside was like the moon - a mirror for the light of the sun and stars, changing color and tone as the sun moved its face. The concave vault and convex dome…is as the sun and the moon. By imitation, the Bird Wings follow with a geometric convex /concave soaring-rhythm in its flight.

It was agreed by all Conferees that, no temple need be build for them of stones, nor gated with golden gates, but instead they are to worship in thickets of small trees.

It was reported to them by Favid Attar that, "From Libya there came about thirty-thousand Cranes, having swallowed foundation stones. Ten-thousand other storks carried the bricks upward; And water the lap-wings and other water birds carried from below up into the air. …and the mortar? was carried by Herons, in hods. And then the Geese, digging down as if with shovels, got it into the hods, for them, with their feet. And the Ducks carried the bricks in girdles around the waist! And Swallows flew up carrying the mud against its stom-ach! Birds were the carpenters and wise woodpeckers, with their beaks, pecked the gates."

"You have created and founded the most glorious ethereal city," Persuasion noted with a congratulatory note, "what great honor you have earned from Humans."

"There were many passionate admirers and lovers of the new city. Humans had up until this time become crazed with Spartan ways. Now they learn to be Birds. …and do everything for pleasure. **They imitate Birds.** They Fly at Dawn, as we do, then together brood upon archival books; then graze upon steep decrees. Many have been given bird names. The merchant is 'Par-tridge'; and some are called Swallow, Raven, Sheldrake, Jay, and Quail……"

Hope excitedly chirped out, "And on account of the love of birds, all are singing a song, in which a swallow is in the lyrics, and a wild duck, or some goose, or a ring-dove, or just wings, or even some small part of a feather!"

"But one thing I tell you:" he contin-ued. "There are coming here, from there, more than ten-thousand in need of Wings and Taloned Claws. So, you will have to gather Wings from somewhere for the new arrivals!"

"For once they have tasted flight, they will forever walk the earth with their eyes turned sky-ward, for there they have been, and there they will long to return"

Leonardo Da Vinci

Persuasion urged them on, "our work cannot be delayed! As quickly as possible, run in and fill the crates and baskets with Wings; Bring wings and meet me at the gate and I shall receive those who are coming for them."

'Aristophanes, Critique of the Gods'

End of Episode Three

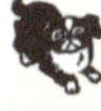

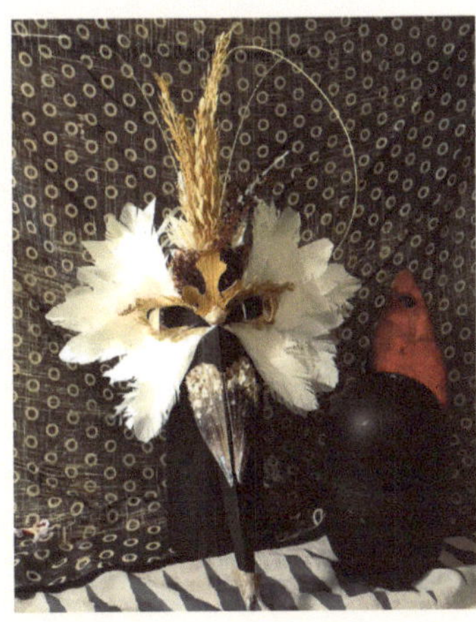

Assignment Five:

Letters

...and the BIRDS could send and carry letters

Assemble letters from sources such as games, signs, type, or others found in your purview and assemble with blocks or spacers to form a composition of related Letters. Draw them in black and white; with light and shadow on Template Two.

Enlarge one study for presentation.

Words

Assemble Letters forming words that are related to one another in a still life format on Template Two. Symbols and related objects in the studio can be added for emphasis of theme. Draw this still life of letters in black and white with color highlights. Enlarge one study for presentation. This can take on the composition of a poster for its image.

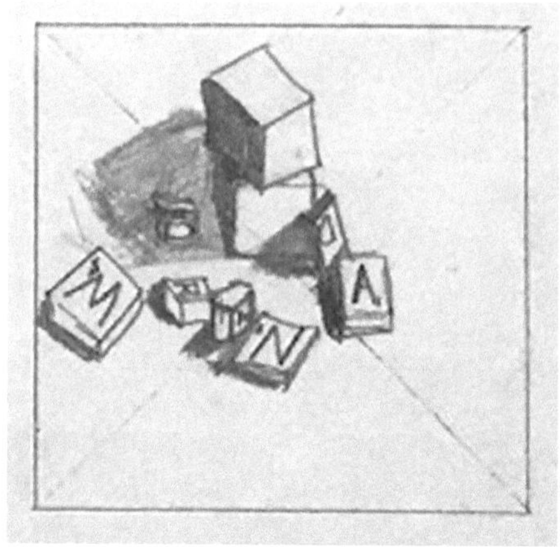

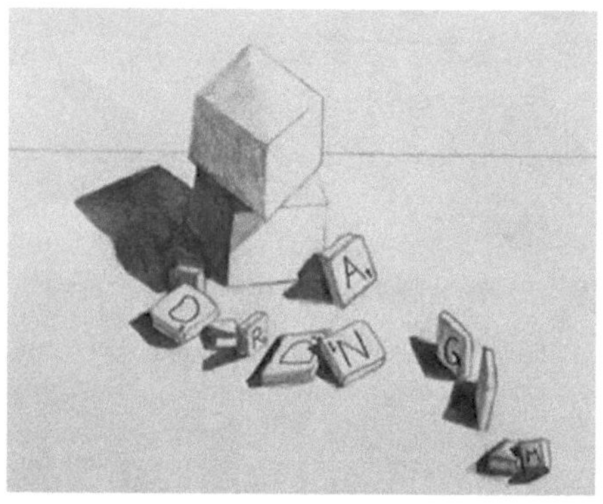

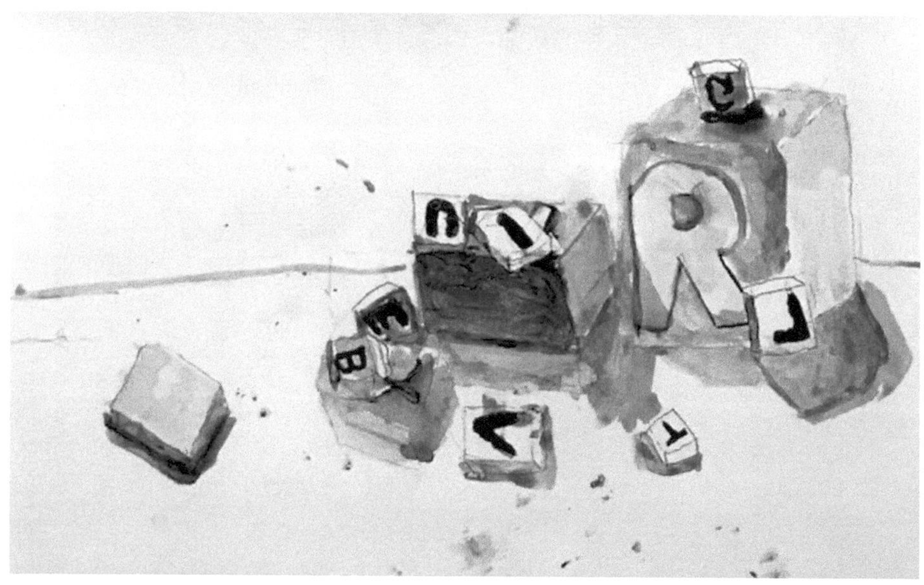

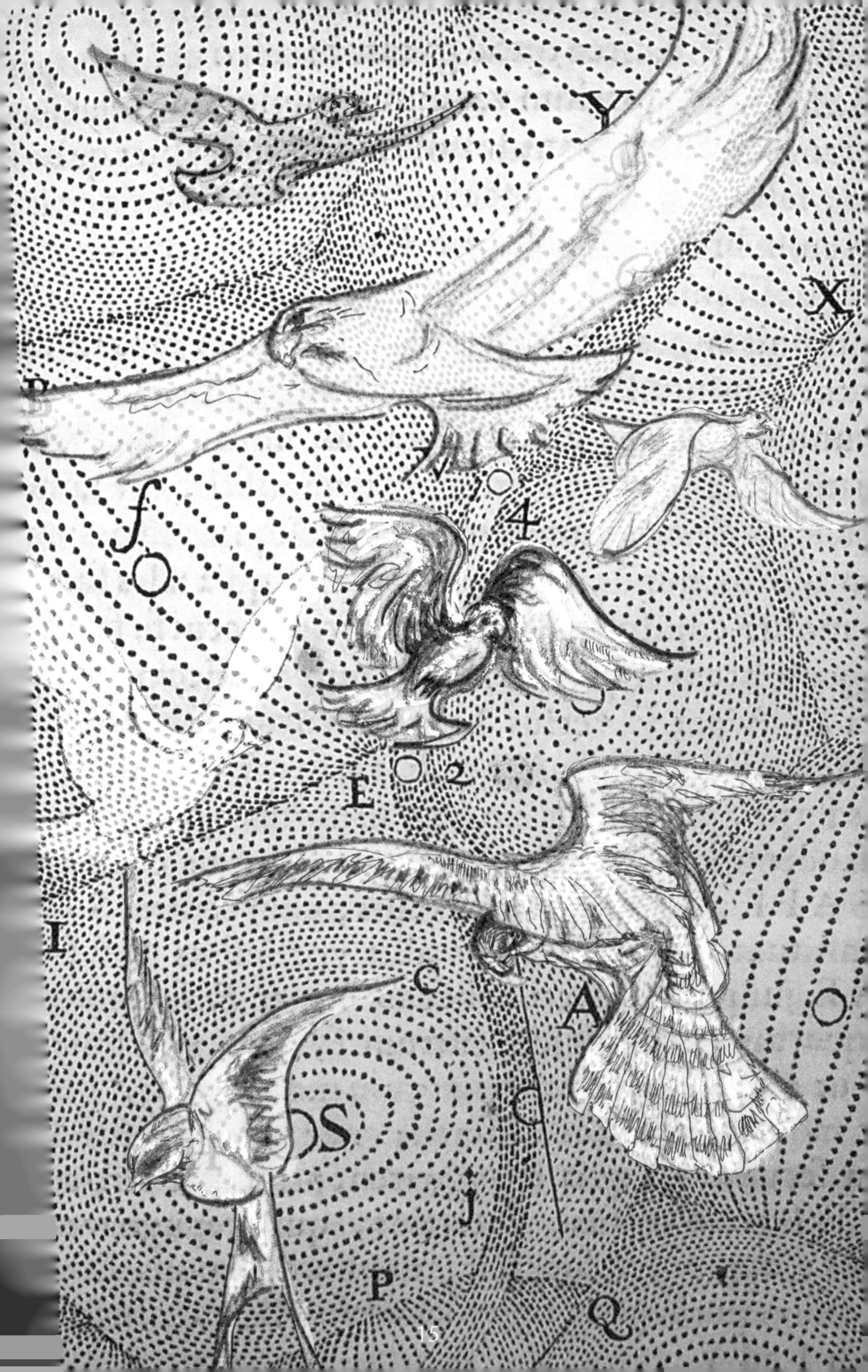

AS THIS, SO THAT

learning to listen, and to see

the Clouds

lines 277-288

Aristophanes, c.447-385bce

Chorus:

Rise, my sisters, Clouds eternal,
Shining bright with morning dew,
From the roaring Ocean's bosom
　To the sky, the world to view.

Let us see the distant mountains
　And the holy earth below,
Where we irrigate the cornfields
　And the babbling rivers flow,
While far off the breakers thunder
　'Neath the sun's unwearied rays:
Make yourselves
　　　　like BIRDlike beings
And to each direct your gaze.

<u>Characters</u>: III
Olympians
Persuasion
Hope
Insightful [Owl]
Longevity [Falcon]
Diligence [Swan]
Adaptive [Crow]
Peaceful [Crane]

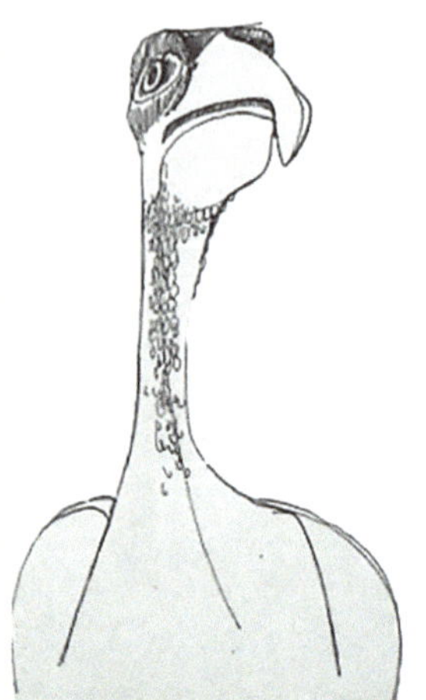

Conference of Birds

concerning the clouds

By proclamation, Persuasion declared, "the world below is inhabited by mortal earthbound Beings* and the heaven above is inhabited by the gods, the Olympians." "The air between," he continued "which holds all in place, spreads between them as a veil of absence. The commanding position of this veil, was destined to be inhabited and superintended by Birds? It is ours."

Hope, invoking some doubt, interjected, "We do not really know if it is our place to seek control of the veil of air until we get there…but we must nevertheless make the journey to ascertain its jurisprudence.

"When the earth and heavens were prepared for habitation, a veil, of intermediate space was spread between

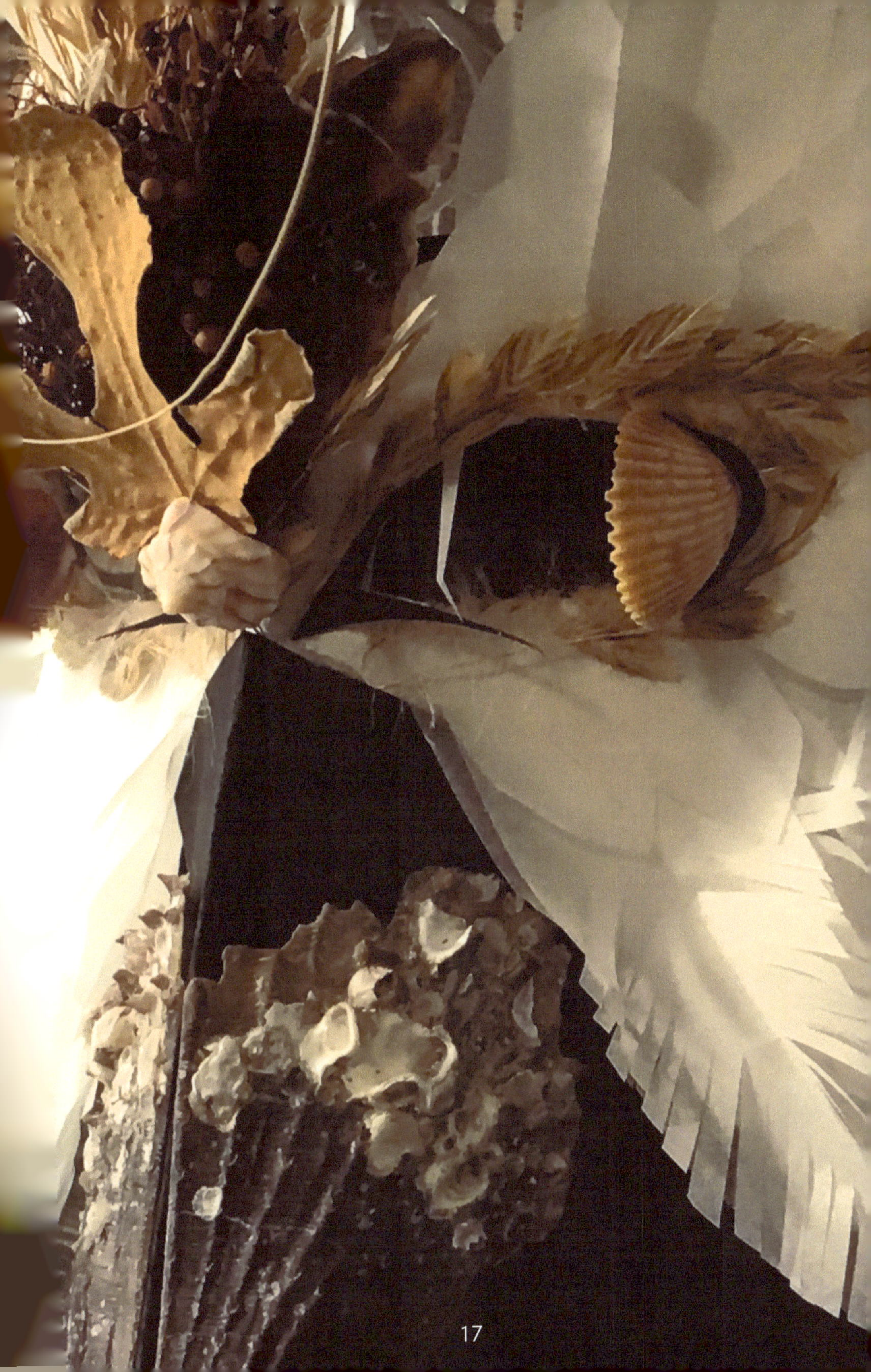

them in darkness. The veil's deep vacuity hung between the burning light above and materiality below. Its Air was spread to appease the semblance of earth bound BEING'S* vicissitudes with the unendurable glory and changeless notions of those heavenly."

Persuasion continued, " It was a veil to appease and subdue the stability and insensibility of the earth's inhabitants below and the immortal passions above.

A new class of sedulous Beings with Wings, inexplicably appeared. They could fly within, over and under the veil. Their miraculous appearance inspired the idea of 'aeronautic' thought. Consequently, this roused a yearning desire for Wings by all Beings".

Insightful, the Owl, hooted an explanation, "Between earth and its Beings arose the Leaf. Between heaven and earth came the Cloud. The earthbound Being was the fallen leaf. The Olympian god was the hidden face peering out over the Clouds flying vapors, observing that leaf's endurance."

The Falcon, as Longevity's shriek, was heard blurting out, "Behold the Cloud! Its form, as far as life's vision can trace it, is of eternal decay…No eyes have ever seen its substance, it being imperfect in its moderation of endurance and obliteration".

Diligence, the questioning Swan cautioned "How then can we anchor our city to a flying vapor of Clouds?"

Hope responded to Diligence excitedly " A feather once fell from the Clouds. It fell somewhere in China. We are not exactly sure where in China. We take that as a sign for us to search for the Truth of its origination in order to answer the Swan.

chorus: "Between heaven and the earth came the falling Feather."

Adaptive, the Crow, set about to herd the Birds from deliberation to usefulness. "Undertaking this mission" he began, "there are among us some Birds with professed capability to see and willingness to be 'seers'. There are talkers, referred to as 'prophets'. "There are also " he noted as an aside, "false seers' … 'the unseeing', and 'false speakers'… those unspeaking on the negative side of silence. There are those Birds who profess the claim to make things,

---

** BEINGS: the widest of categories; anything that exists or is conceived as having existence, which can SEE, COMMUNICATE and BREATH [mortal, earth-bound, or immortal]. BEINGS embrace their origin, their genesis, in either nature or in the genesis of the supernatural [an ethereal nature]. Birds, as well as Humans, are mortal-Beings. Gods, and the here-to-for referred to Olympians are immortal-Beings.*

manufactured out of notions…called 'poets'. The most dangerous Birds are believed to be 'thinkers' … known on occasion to be 'philosophers'. To build our city, all Birds have to agree to share the responsibilities of 'workers' as well as just being 'thinkers'', seers'', talkers', 'poets' or 'philosophers' …"

"They are one and the same" interrupted Hope, "as the workers aught to be thinking and the thinkers aught to be working."

"Now" insisted Insightful, the Owl "separating or dividing birds into attitudinal or altitudinal differences will not serve to unify us in positioning our city. We are a winged heterogeneous ornithological community … destined to establish our city in the Clouds."

"We must watch for the whispering-winds-watch-word for direction," Longevity screeched from a perch. Crane peacefully nodded its head as if in blessing.

Amen!

End of Episode Four

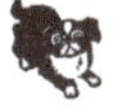

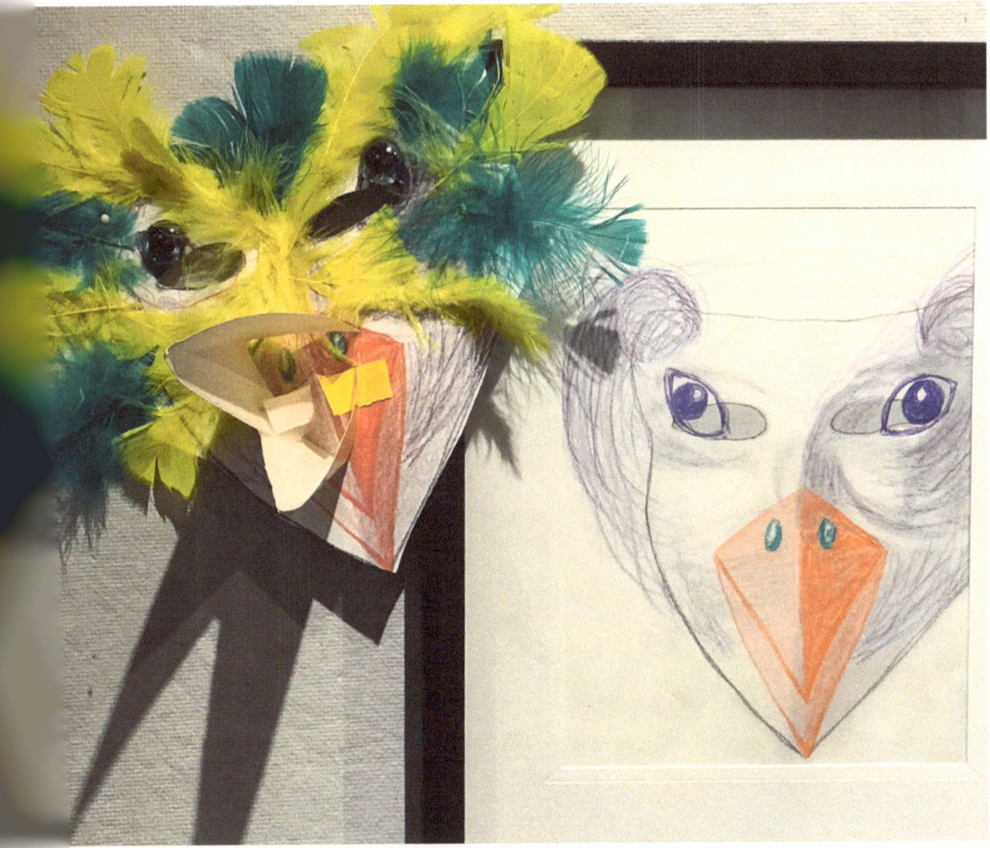

Assignment Six:

A. Draw a Mask of Your Bird.
   Draw a white generic Mask [available at Michaels or equal] and follow the instructions below.

1. On a **first** piece of transparent paper: Add/Draw **two eyes** for the Bird so that it will be able to see with and through them. They must be set in the mask so that they enhance the aero-dynamics of the head. Note the side location of the Birds eyes.

2. On a **second** piece of transparent paper: Add/Draw **two ears** for the BIRD to allow spacial perception of longitude and latitude and its direction and altitude.

3. On a **third** piece of transparent paper: Add/Draw one mouth so that it has the potential for speech outward and nurturing inward.

4. On a **fourth** piece of transparent paper: Add/Draw the bird's beak with **two nostrils**, to enable the transfer of air and spirit as it measures time in units of breath.

5. On a **fifth** piece of transparent paper: [11x14] **Draw all of the above**, one on top of the others… each with its own separate color. This collage of elements will represent the soulful existence of your BIRD … as a MASK

6. NOW Build the MASK, in three dimensions, so that it can be donned by you when delivering your oration at the next Conference of Birds.

The generic mask is for use as an armature for the actual mask. It can be made of scored matt board, cast-plaster with mesh reinforcing, or linen coated with plaster. The MASK…. must be wearable.

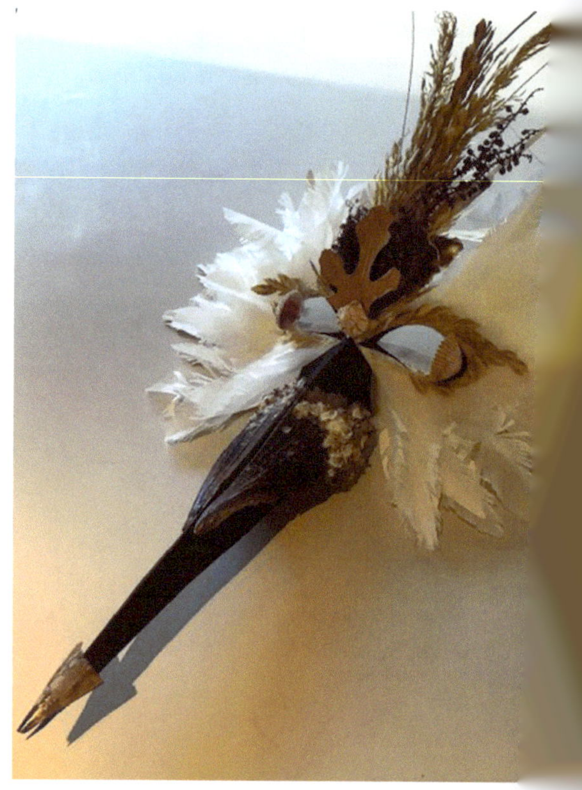

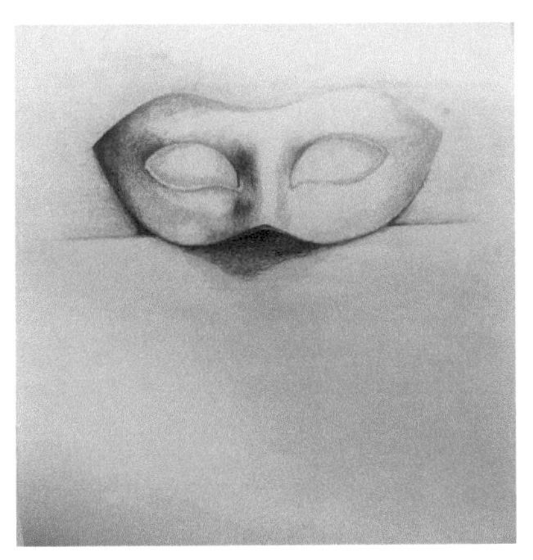
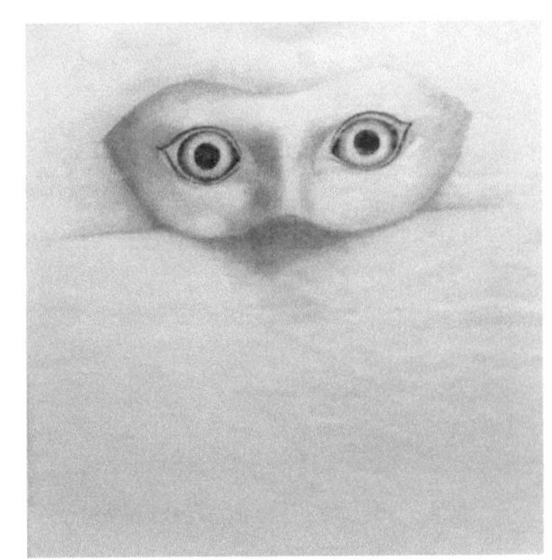
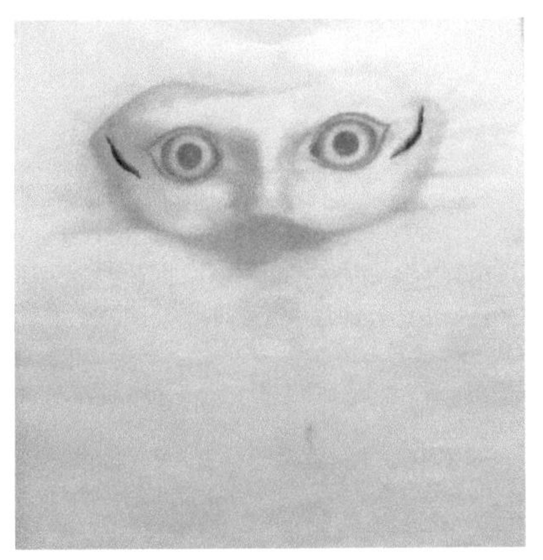
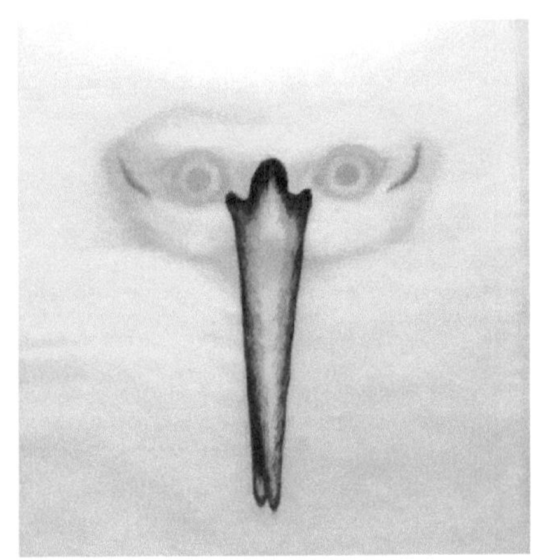
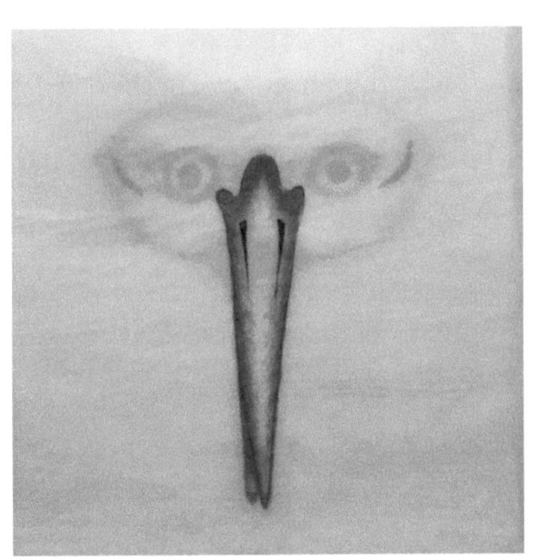
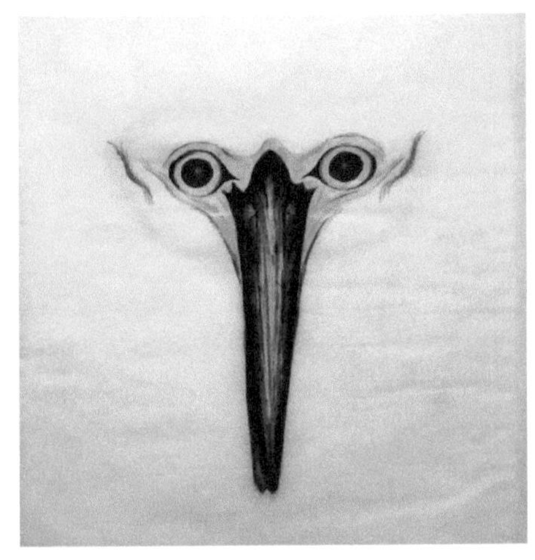

AS THIS, SO THAT

learning to listen, and to see

The Search for Wisdom

the wisdom of BenSira

[14:20-14:27] 273 bce

Happy is the person who meditates on Wisdom,
 and fixes his gaze on understanding;

Who ponders her ways in his heart
and pays attention to her paths,

Pursuing her like a scout
and watching her entryways;

Who peeps through her window
and listens at her doors;

Who encamps near her house
 and fastens his tent pegs next to her walls;

Who pitches his tent beside her
 and lives as her welcome neighbor;

Who builds his nest in her leafage
 and lodges in her branches;

Who takes refuge from the heat in her shade
and dwells in her home.

Characters: IV

Tereus the Hoopoe

Insight, the Owl

Lady and Queen Wisdom

Solomon

Persuasion

Hope

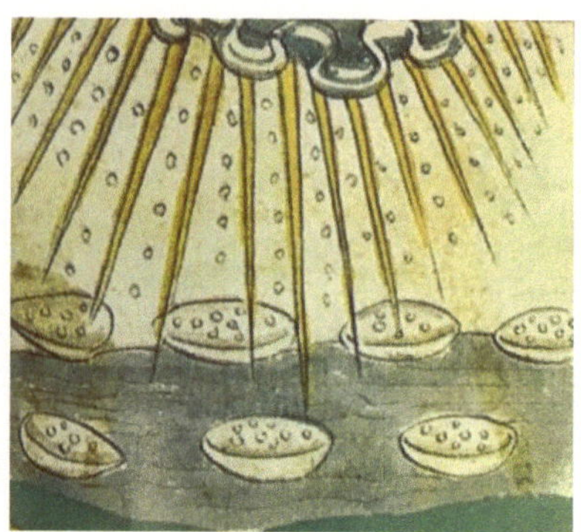

Conference of Birds

the air between

The world below was ruled by Kings, the world above ruled by Gods. Aristophanes' Birds searched for a King. Attar's Birds searched for a God. Our Birds search for a world ruled by Wisdom. A world ruled and guided by the higher power of Insight.

Not all gods, kings or leaders are equal nor necessarily wise, good, or apt in sovereign ways. They are sometimes mis-assigned in their palaver of staged effectuation. Tereus, son of a great King, choosing disgrace rather than Wisdom, tore out Philomela's tongue after defiling her. He was, consequently, turned into a Hoopoe, of the Hawk variety, in retribution. [Ovid, Metamorphosis 6.438-674] Philomela was turned into a nightingale,
…a voice in darkness forever.

Tereus stepped from behind the Rock presenting himself to Persuasion and Hope as the promised ONE, who could lead in commandeering the domain of the Veil-of-Air by engaging the pinioned wing of a Hoopoe. [see vol.1] The Hoopoe, crowned with a stiff brightly colored crest and a beak as long and protruded as a lance … was a harbinger of evil and bird of war. Both Aristophanes and Attar, poets of antiquities great comedies, chose the Hoopoe to lead their Birds expedition as a ploy to satirically ridicule the prevalent vices and follies of their time. It was said by some that Solomon too had satirically crowned the Hoopoe "for its wisdom in refusing to pay homage to women".

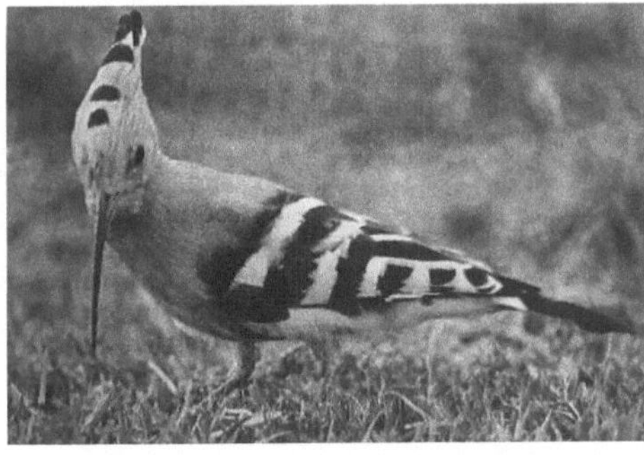

Solomon's messenger, the Hoopoe, on his mission to find hidden knowledge for the King…reported the discovery of a wise and powerfully wealthy Queen named Sheba, who ruled a magnificent kingdom. Solomon was led to believe that this Queen worshipped the Sun. He invited her to relinquish her worships adoration and share his majestic Kingdom, and thereby build upon his growing wisdom. Not daunted by his generous offer she chose to remain in her own domain … not to worship the Sun, but rather to venerate its initiation, as originator, of the Light of Mortal Vision.

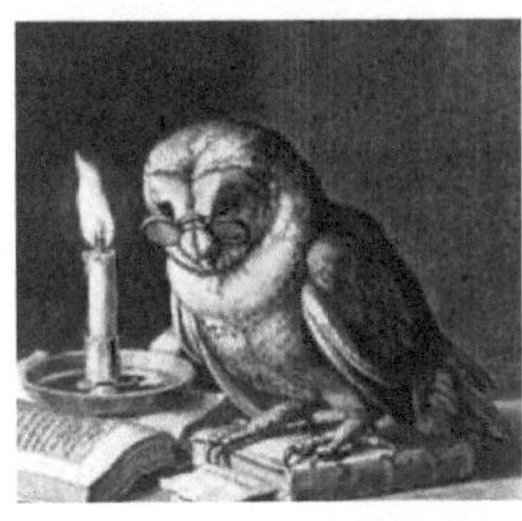

This Queen of Wisdom laid claim to eternity, forward and backward. [Sirach 24]; She was a teacher who showed the way and like her pet Owl, was known to be both a thinker and hunter. She was a conjurer of plans of strategy in lieu of those of brute force or defilement. Known to be the guardian of memory, she caused deep introspection to align with true intention. With her ability to see in the dark she taught lessons of clarity and deception. As a mentor, she set the example of an observant, calm, majestic and calculated pathfinder. Her complemental pet Owl had, unlike other birds, both eyes set forward, enabling them to view objects with both eyes at once. Janus like, the Owl was able to see, within one threshold, both forward and backward.

Wisdom and her seemingly sacred Owl were esteemed for their regal silence, wisdom, and fierce intelligence. It was decided by the congregating Birds to be fitting for the Owl to lead them in their mission. All agreed that the world they sought was one ruled by Wisdom as a fitting place of rest and foundation for their future habitation…They trusted that the prescience of the Owl would guide them to its whereabouts.

The search and its democratic con-fabulation was commandeered by the Owl; Insight. By fiat she overruled the choice of the Hoopoe, in guid-ance and ascendency. Plans for the setting of foundations to build their city upon [or suspended beneath] were enthusiastically launched. Words, hoots and chirps were freely exchanged by the contemplative congregants relative to aspirations, objections and excuses.

The Hoopoe, of historic idiosyncratic tendency, commenced the proceed-ings by passing the gavel to Wisdom's Owl.

The Birds assembled in anticipation. All praised the splendor of the imag-ined distant Place. All rose impatient to be on the wing. However, when they pondered the journey's length, they hesitated and then declined - each according to its kinds [cooked up] Excuse. We heard first from the finch, parrot, partridge, falcon, francolin and nightingale, followed by the peacock, the duck, the homa, the hawk, and then the heron. The Birds Excuses, as they declined participa-tion in this mission, was recounted by Attar.

End of Episode Five

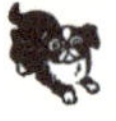

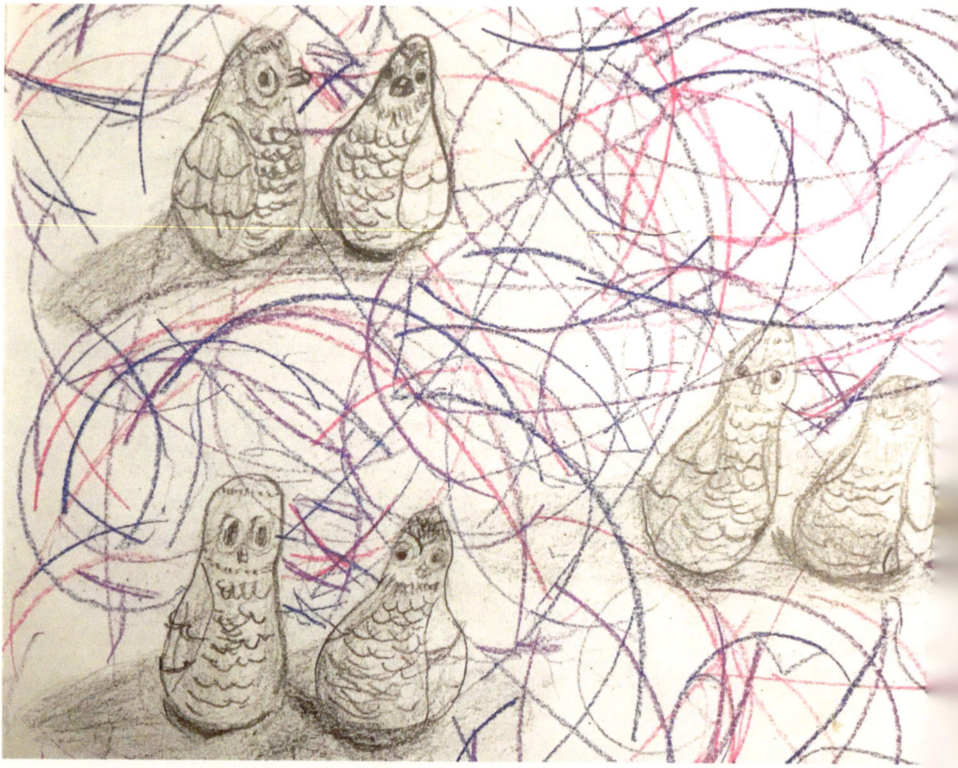

The Bird's Conference opened,

welcoming and introducing the families of Birds.

[from Farid Attar's Conference of Birds - lines 616 - 688 - modified].

Dear Owl, Welcome! You will be our guide.
And you are welcome, finch! Rise up and play.
    Those liquid notes that steal men's
    hearts away.
And welcome, parrot, perched in paradise!
    Your splendid plumage bears a strange
    device.
Welcome, dear partridge how you strut with
    pride
    Along the slopes of wisdom's mountain
    side.
Rare falcon, welcome! How long will you be
    So fiercely jealous of your liberty?
And welcome, francolin! Since once you heard
    And answered The first all-commanding
    word.
Welcome, dear nightingale from your sweet
    throat
    Pour out the pain of lovers note by note.
And welcome, peacock - once of paradise
    Who let the venomous, smooth snake
    entice
    Your instincts to its masters evil vice.
Cock pheasant, welcome! With your piercing
    sight,
    Look up and see the heart's source
    drowned in light.
Dear pigeon, welcome with what joy you yearn
    To fly away, how sadly you return!
Welcome, sweet turtle-dove and softly coo
    Until the heavens scatter jewels on you-
And welcome, hawk! Your flight is high and
    proud,
    But you return with head politely bowed -
And little goldfinch, welcome! May your fire
    Be an external sign of fierce desire.

Assignment Seven:
Welcoming a New Year

Acknowledge the welcoming of the New Year 2021 with a suitable celebratory Drawing of the convex/concave stroke of your birds wings in flight … or a masked self portrait.

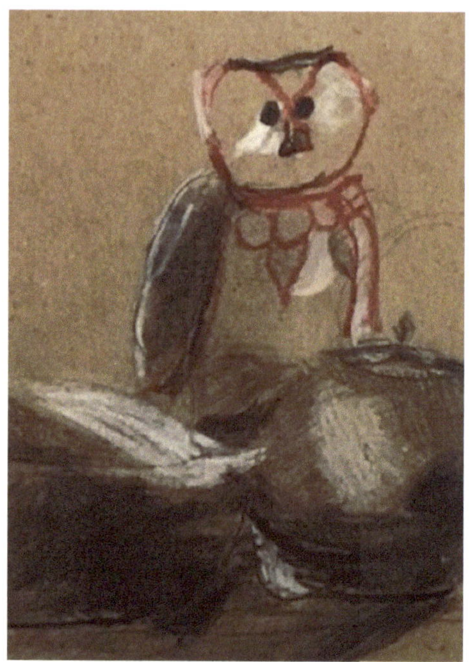

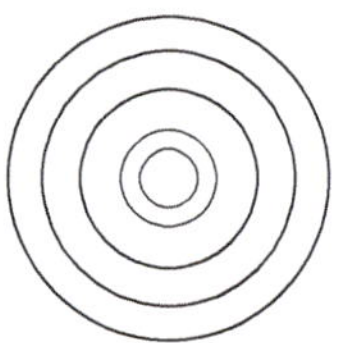

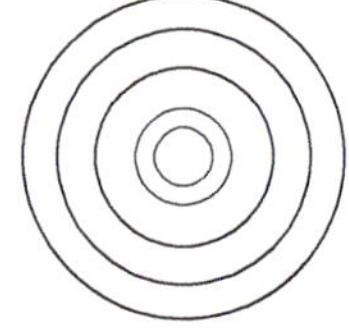

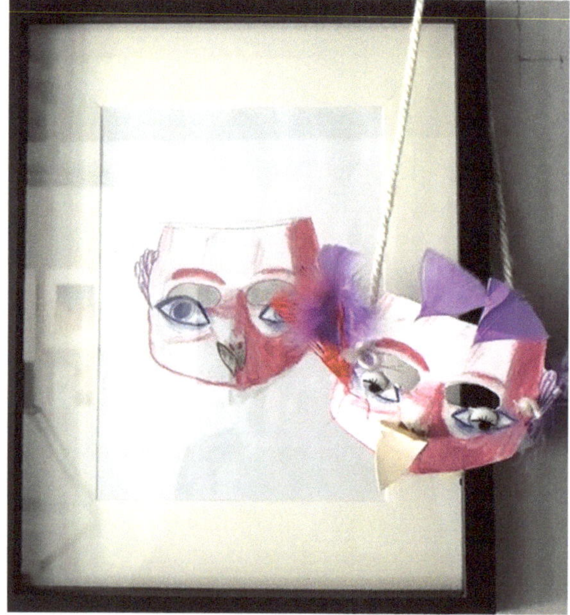

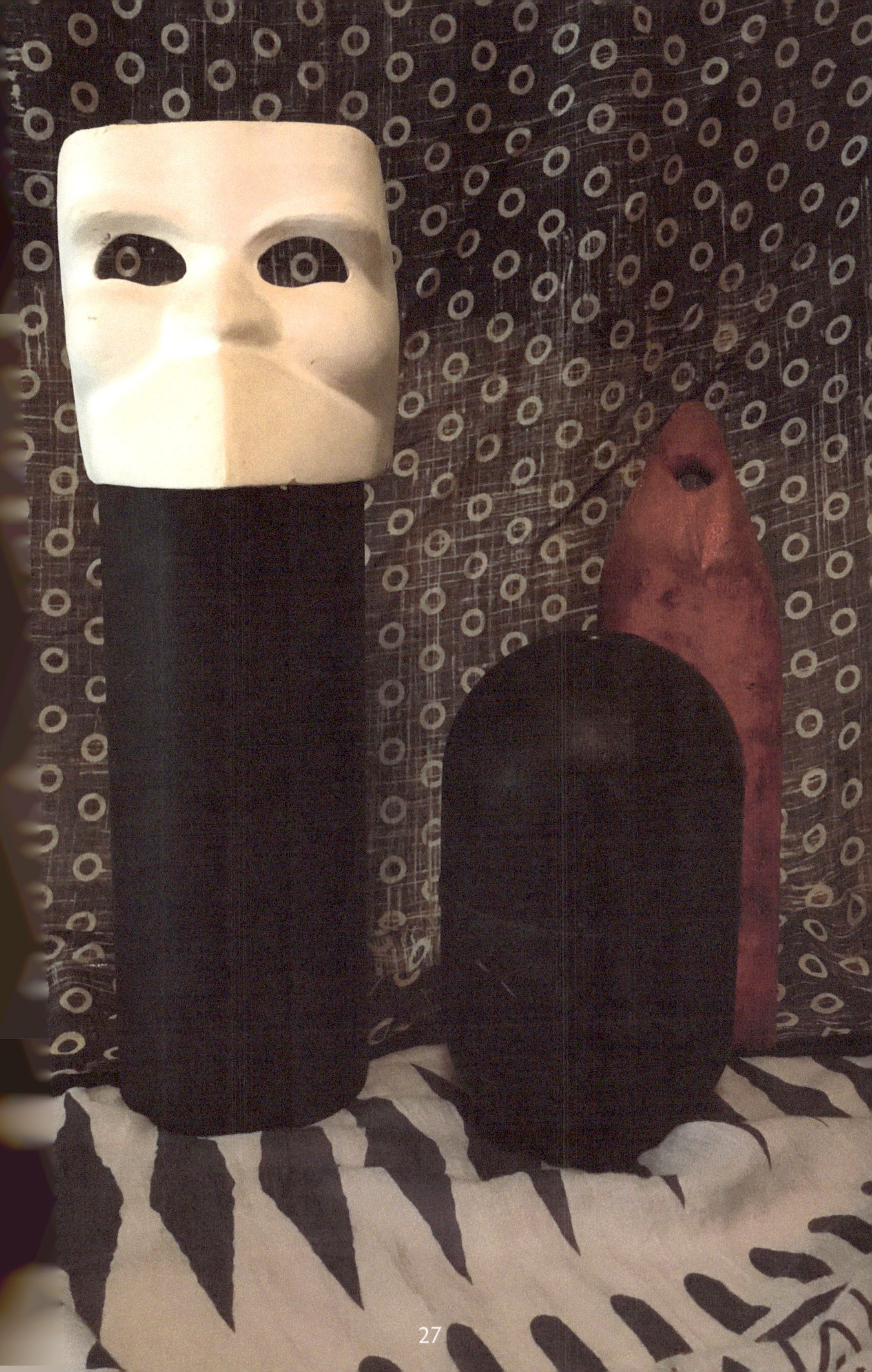

AS THIS, SO THAT
learning to listen, to see, and to focus

Abt Vogler IV

Robert Browning

And the emulous heaven
yearned down, and made
effort to reach the earth,

As the earth had done her
best, in my passion to
scale the sky:

Novel splendors burst forth,
grew familiar and dwelt with
mine,

Not a point nor peak but
found and fixed its
wandering star;

Meteor-moons of blaze: and
they did not pale or
pine,

For earth had attained to
heaven, there was no more
near or far.

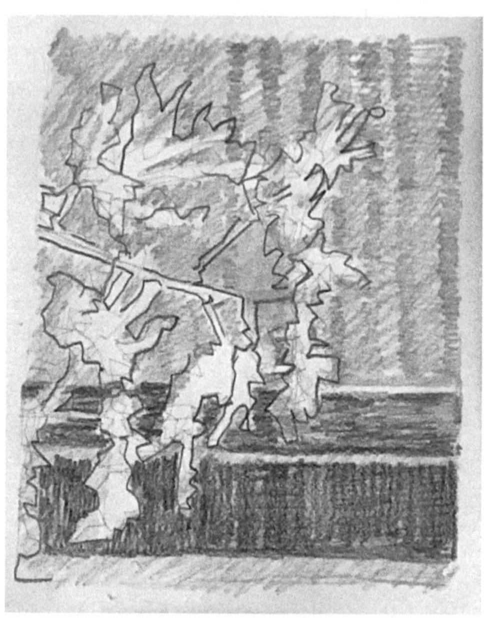

Conference of Birds

*One touch of nature makes all the
world akin...*

A.E. Abbott

Owl convened the Conference of Birds
comparing the outcomes of similar en-
deavors from antiquity, by citing biblical
metaphors.

"Abraham," she began "in naming a
singular invisible Creator, GOD, brought
both unity and strife to an uncertain
world." Continuing chronologically she
explained, " Complaints of insufficiency
of that unpredictable-invisible-sover-
eign, by and by, brought demands for
a mortal KING. A King who bore recog-
nizable foibles and strengths of their

own kind. First, and unbeknownst to them, they chose a slipshod King, named Saul. Following Saul's craven demise they replaced him by another, a romantic but heroic war-mongering King, David."

"The proof text of this axiom"

Persuasion offered, "enables us to embark upon a hearing of consensus by participating Birds. A census of all who stand with us in:

"The enactment and establishment of our new City under the tutelage of Insight, the Owl. ....

chorus:

"Now, how to Pass the gavel from a Creator, to a Hoopoe, [a Bird of war], and then to an Owl with enviable Wisdom. A Creator is not equal to a Destroyer, is not equal to a Conciliator. Neither alone is able to sustain equilibrium. In mathematics this may resemble the 'scalene' triangle of three unequal legs. It is difficult to advance on any path with three unequal legs without a walking stick or Carrolls 'walking-stick-of-destiny'. Wisdom, as a conciliator and a most congenial sovereign, was known to be capable of imparting that stabilizing stick by degree or decree of influence. Thus, the choice of Wise Solomon came to pass, as the inheriting son of David and Creation itself."*

[walking stick of destiny as a variable hypotenuse.]*

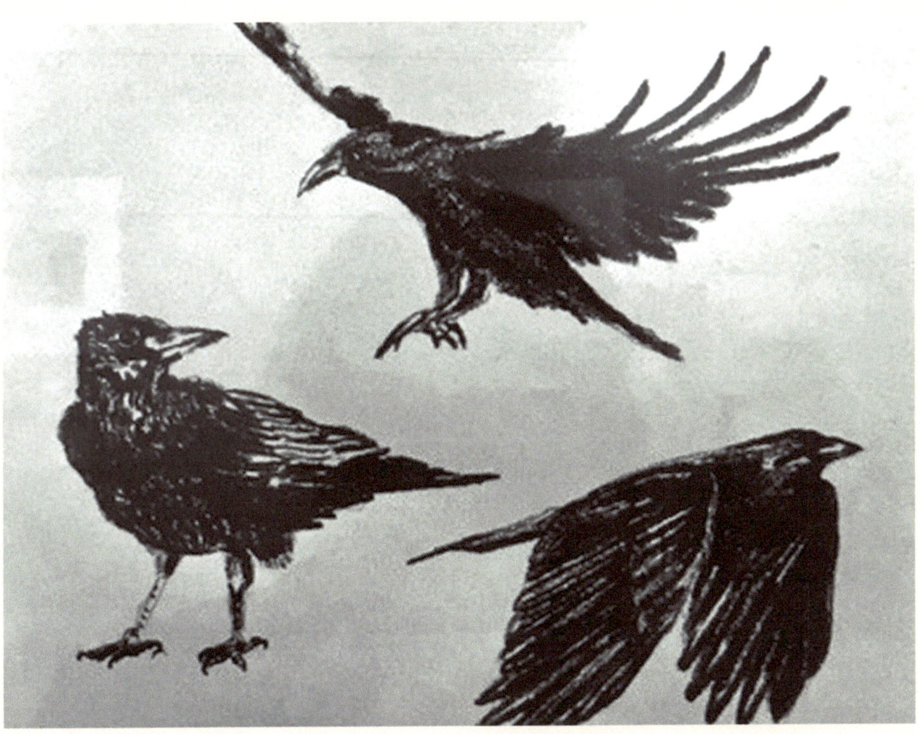

Do we hear Ayes?"

To Persuasions chagrin many Birds unexpectedly declined participation in the proposed mission. Their Objections, more likened to Excuses, are here recounted, clarified and modified reflecting accounts by our scribe *Farid Attar* in his own words.

the nightingale spoke first:

'The secrets of all love are known to me. My songs are the sweetest notes of the melancholy Lute, and the plaintive wailing of the lovesick Flute. My love is here. The journey you propose cannot distract me from my life - my Rose. Her buds are mine, she blossoms in my sight. How could I leave her for a single night?'

the parrot:

'I have been caged as a cringing slave by heartless men. My desire is to be free again. If I could reassert my liberty, I'd find the stream of immortality. That stream could content my thirsting soul. I have no wish to seek the airy throne of which you speak of as a goal.'

the peacock:

'The painter of the world created me, in multi-colored pomp, and placed me as a dweller in my Paradise. There is one fixed goal which I can understand. My dearest hope is that some blessed day a guide will come to show the way of my return home. An airy throne of a Place above as a goal for me is too unknown. My inward gaze is fixed forever on that lovely land … remembered as 'my Paradise' and home.'

"Of all vain things EXCUSES are the vainest"

Buxton

the duck:

'Purity like mine is hard to find. My soul and feathers are spotless and defined. I live on water, the source of everything that lives. I cannot go places where no streams or rivers flow. They tend to wash away the world of discontent. Why should I leave this perfect element?'

the partridge:

'My one desire is Jewels. I pick through quarries for their fire. You cannot fight with one who sleeps and feeds on precious stones, and is convinced he needs no other goal in life. To yearn for something other than a Jewel is to desire what dies – to be a fool. I must discover precious stones or die. My life is here and I have no wish to fly.'

the homa:

'What is a homa?

It is a Bird whose shadow heralds majesty. A mythical Bird whose shadow, when it falls on a human, indicates that he or she is destined to be King or Queen. Who else can look down as one whose shadow brings the royal crown. Who then could look UP to cast its shadow?

The world should bask on my magnificence. I need not search for the relevance of reverence above.'

the hawk:

'My eyes are hooded and I cannot see. But I perch proudly on my sovereigns wrist. A seed from my sovereigns hand is all I need. The eminence I have suffices me. I cannot travel. I prefer to be perched on the royal wrist than to be struggling through some world or other with no end point in view.'

the heron:

'My misery prefers the empty shoreline of the sea. My love is for the ocean, but since I, a Bird, must be excluded from the deep, I haunt the solitary shore and weep. I cannot join you in an arduous quest as my love is fixed entirely on the lips of the sea.'

the finch:

'I am less sturdy than a 'hair' and lack the courage that my betters share. Oh, great distance to the desired sanctuary … how could a sickly creature stand alone before this proposed drudgery. I cannot join this delusive race…exhaustion would cut short my pace. Joseph was hidden in a well, I seek my destiny in a gentle dell'

End of Episode Six

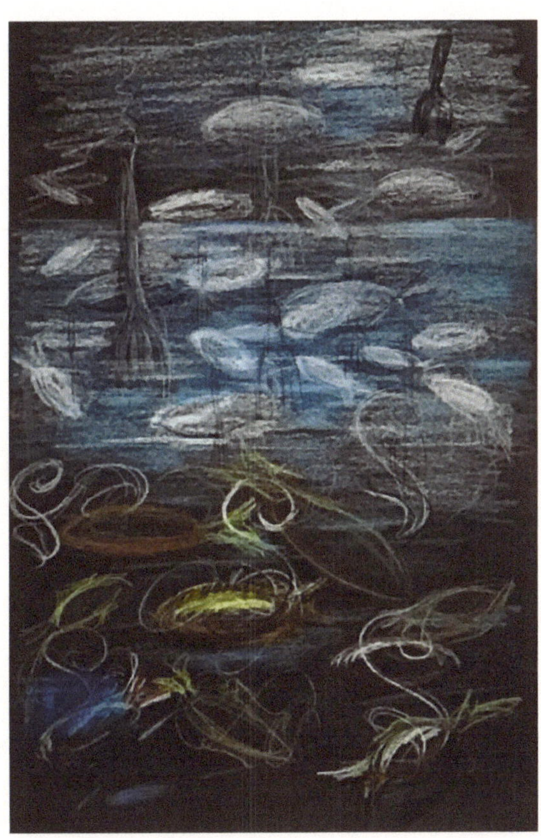

Assignment Eight:

Write, in one or more paragraphs, the EXCUSE your Bird offers for not taking flight … or you … by-way-of not taking Drawing Assignments!!!!

Propose the Owl's possible answers to each Bird's reluctance to break with its earthbound attachments.

DRAW the element the Bird is most attached to in its earthly existence from which it fears to part.

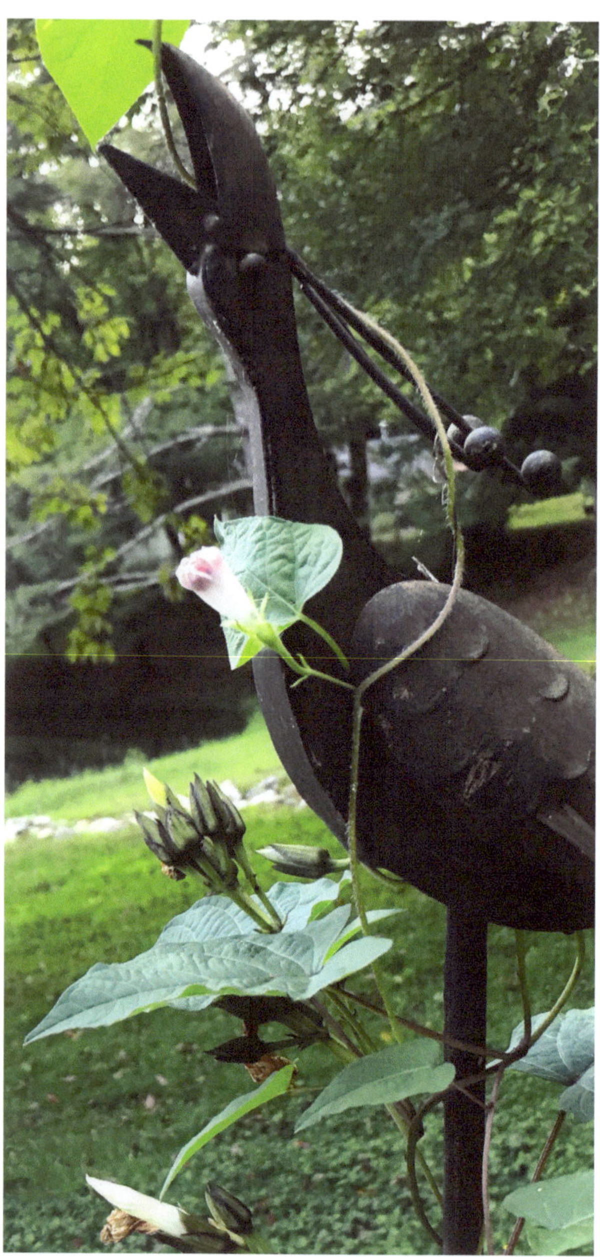

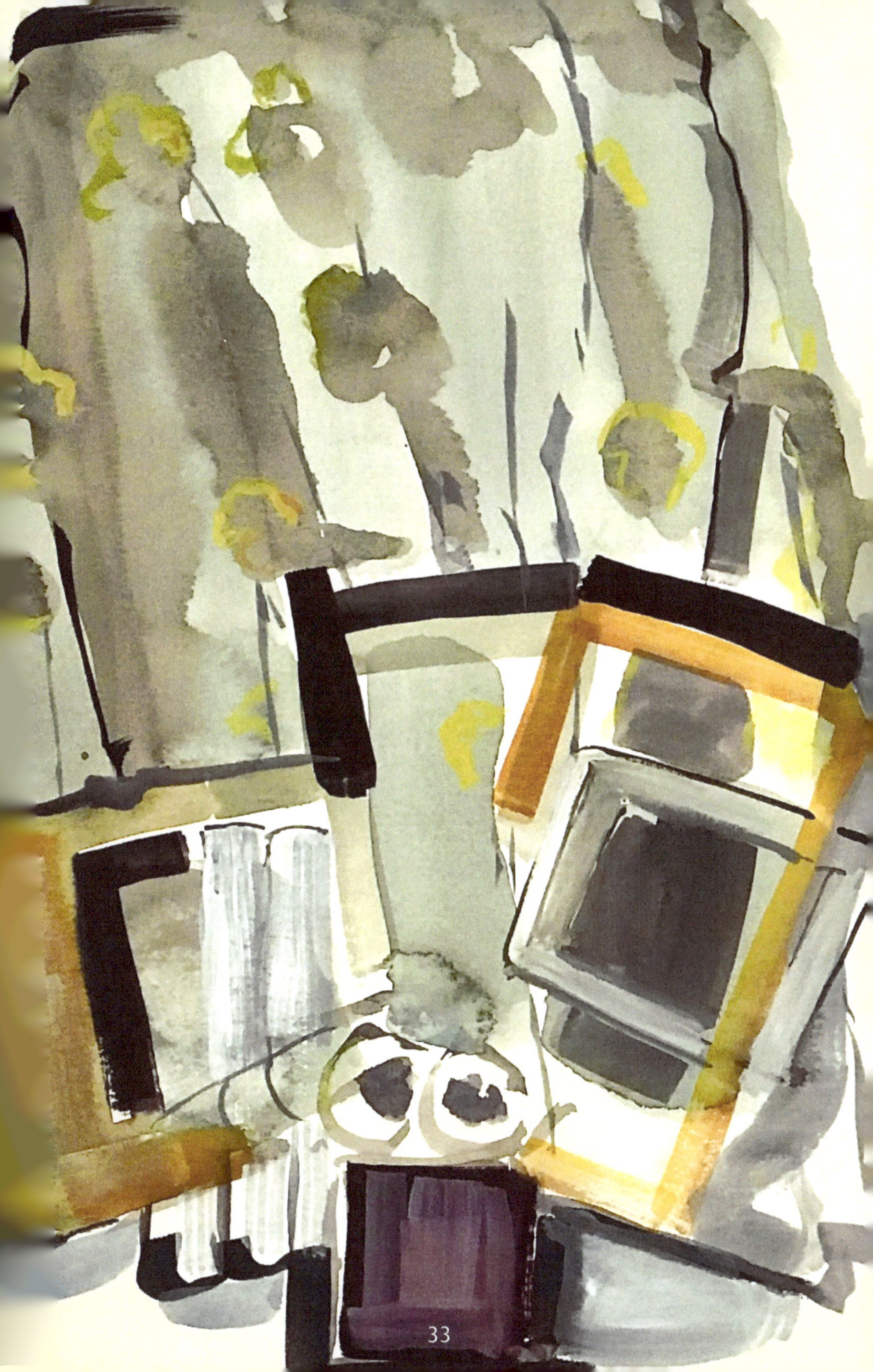

AS THIS, SO THAT

learning to listen, to see, and to focus

Flatland Dedicatory

Edwin A. Abbott

To
The inhabitants of Space in
GENERAL
And its High Council in
PARTICULAR
This Work is Dedicated By a
Humble Native of
FLATLAND
In the Hope that
Even as she was Initiated into
the Mysteries
of THREE DIMENSIONS
Having been previously
conversant with
ONLY TWO
The citizens of that Celestial
Region
May aspire yet higher and
higher
To the Secrets
of
FOUR FIVE OR EVEN SIX
      DIMENSIONS

Thereby contributing
To the Enlargement
of IMAGINATION
And the possible
Development
Of that most rare and
excellent Gift
of MODESTY
Among the Superior Minds
of SOLID HUMANITY

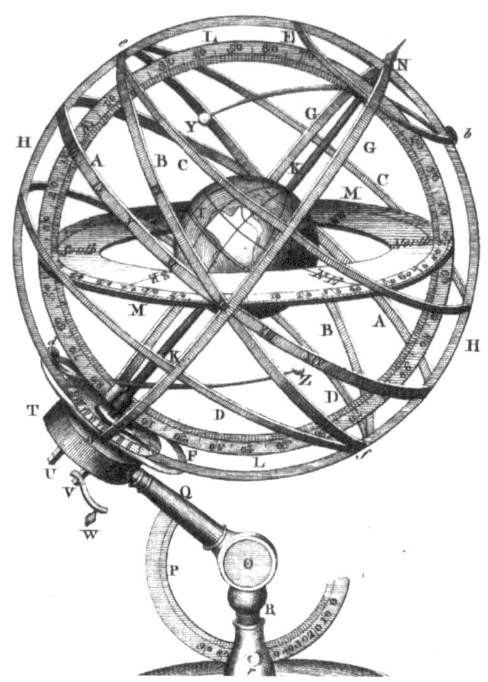

Conference of Birds

The flight of a bird is measureless. It
charts its path in song, catches fare under
its wing, coasts air-drafts, connects floral
pistil points, and trespasses parallel
and diverging cirrus fibers through the
legionary nautical constellations of stars
to fulfill its ambition.

*"It becomes 'part' of the great drama
in the procession of the constellations as if it were a gigantic circus
parade."*

Julia Diggens

Omnivigant, wandering in all directions,
it occasionally holds a stilled wing in flight
above the terrestrial landscape so as to

find *"one touch of Nature's wisdom that makes the whole world kin…."*

Wm. Shakespeare, Troilus and Cressida

The Space of its flight is actually, in fact, THOUGHTLAND. There it can see, with its mind's eye, the inside of all solid things. See, to recognize all essences without need of measure. Within its sight, a cube can move in a new direction making every particle of its interior pass through a new kind of space … creating a more perfect perfection of itself.

In order to undertake this flight and allow the Birds to successfully plan their city in space, tools-for-orientation and defining-of-concepts of interrelationships are needed. To establish the where of things, the how, the why and what of things in space, descriptive terms are needed.

Persuasion and Hope agreed upon five basic spatial concepts* to open its conference of Birds dialogue.

Hope tended toward favoring demonstrations, of what was uncontrovertibly seen as known to be TRUE. Persuasion favored dealing with the PROBABLE or PLAUSIBLE.

Their difference being one favoring strict-demonstration as opposed to the other favoring persuasion-by-argument. Basically, this centered around HAVING knowledge, in lieu of having a THEORY about it.

Alighting, 'with a piece of string, a straight edge and a shadow' we will, as real or imagined Birds, embark upon our first lesson in charting the Forms and Foundation of the proposed aerial cityscape. We will begin by fabricating simple forms in the air, folded into and relying on a gravitation-less sky. We will gather from our environment three tools for construction … paper, X-acto knife, glue … and four tools for documentation and coordination … paper, pencil, light and shadow.

One could inquire as to how a Bird, having no hands, could possibly use all these tools. We know that they have many sophisticated skills … like weaving nests while hanging upside down from the branch of a tree. We can assume they have had to develop basic skills in order to conceive of, much less utilize, the warp and wefts of inverted weaving in unstructured space. We will understand these skills once we thoughtfully begin problem solving ourselves … with axioms and maxioms.

***Pointland**: no dimension

Lineland: one dimension

Flatland: two dimensions

Spaceland: three dimensions

Thoughtland: four dimensions

the 4 dimensions of thought/imagination

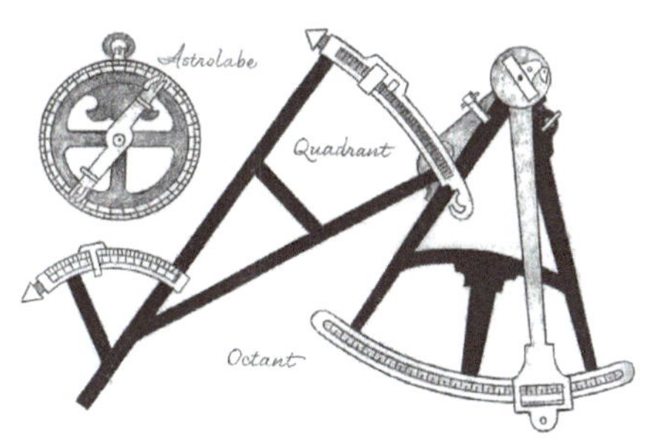

35

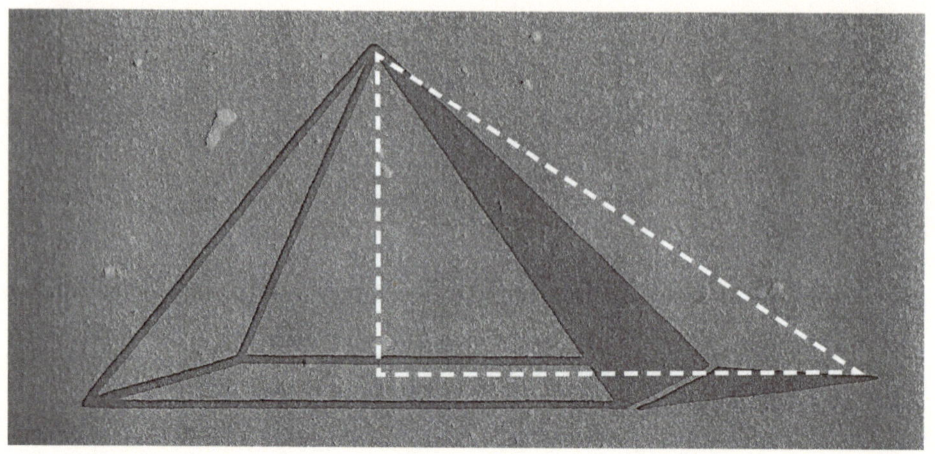

Our first challenge will be the construction of the pyramid… four sided and the simplest 3-Dimensional configuration. For this I have attached a TEMPLATE to be cut, scored and folded. Before glueing it together experiment with three more construction trials of the form. Arrange these four folded pyramids… on a mirrored surface. Leaving parts [sides] of them open, Draw the space captured within their four planes…that you can see.

Now glue all the pyramids together and arrange them in another composition on the mirrored surface with shades and shadows [no lines]. With a red dotted line imply the spaces within…which will serve its nesting chicks.

End of Episode Seven

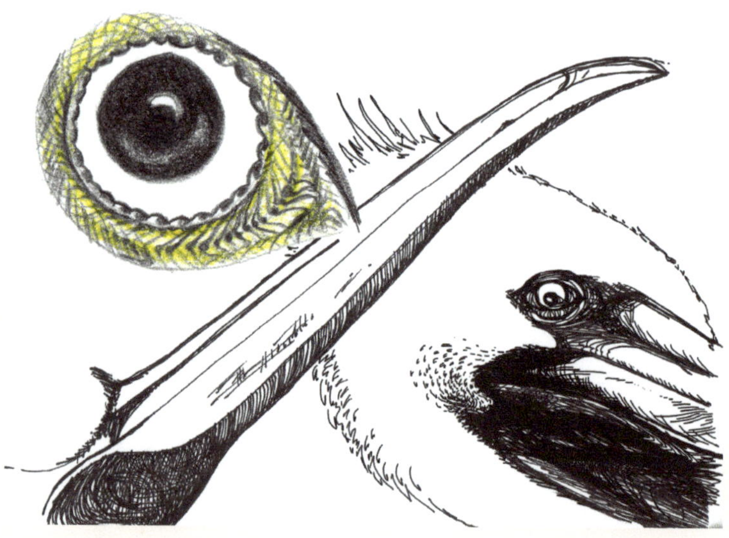

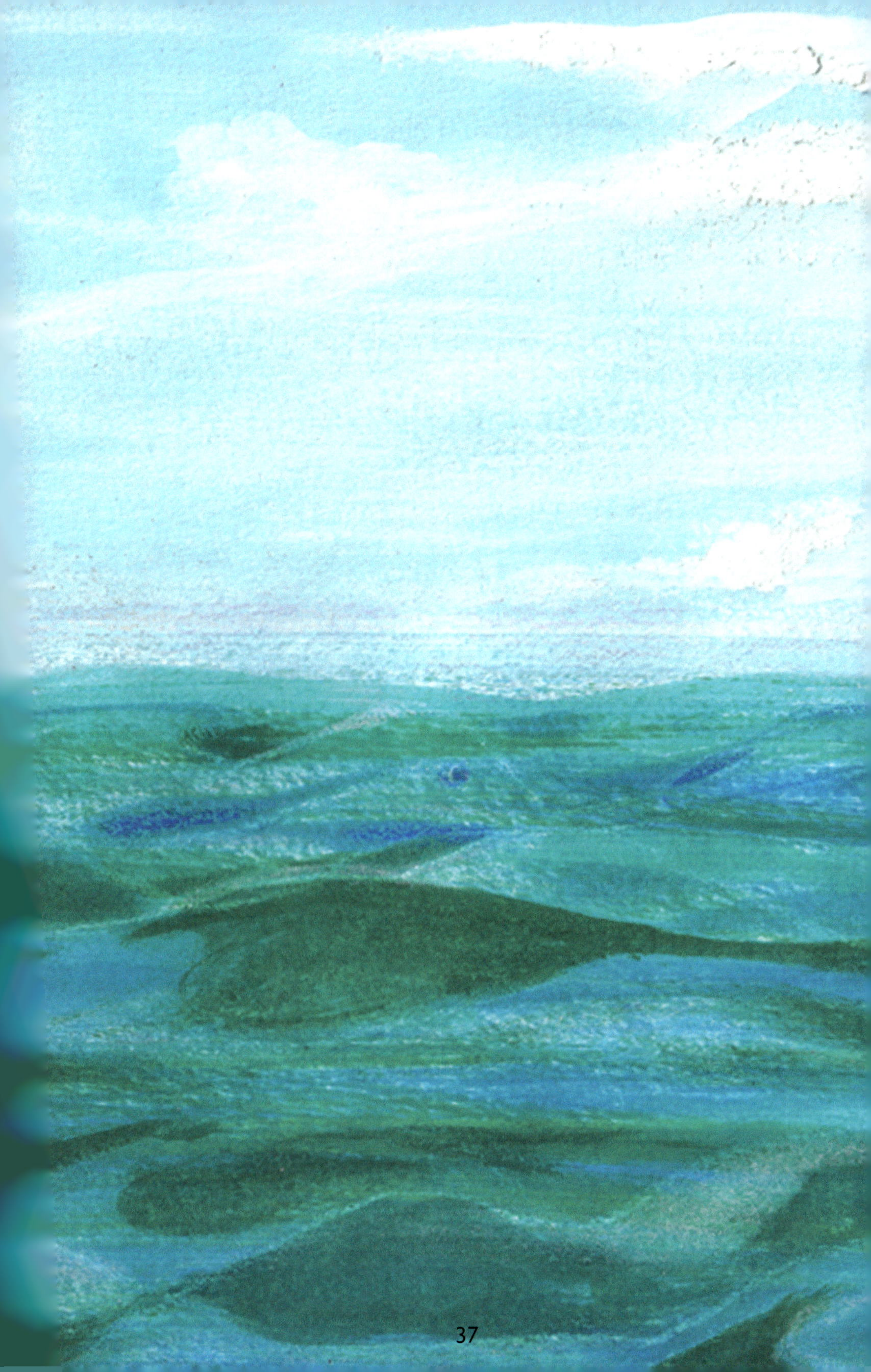

Assignment Nine:
The first descriptive geometry lesson

that those of antiquity failed to qual-ify by not completing their DRAW-ING prerequisites. [see vol.2: one cannot measure the sky with a ruler]

There is a DOT locating a place.

Two DOTS connected to signify direction and scale and creating a LINE.

Many DOTS = many lines = connect-ed PLANES suggesting FORM.

Many lines dragged in space form a PLANE.

PLANES joined to PLANES create FORMS.

In order to have a FORM a minimum of four attached Planes are required.

a PYRAMID [Tetrahedron] can be created with four planes, connected and folded.… the pyramid is the most basic geometric FORM with four sides.

FOLD THE PYRAMID

[copy to stiffer paper for ease of folding]

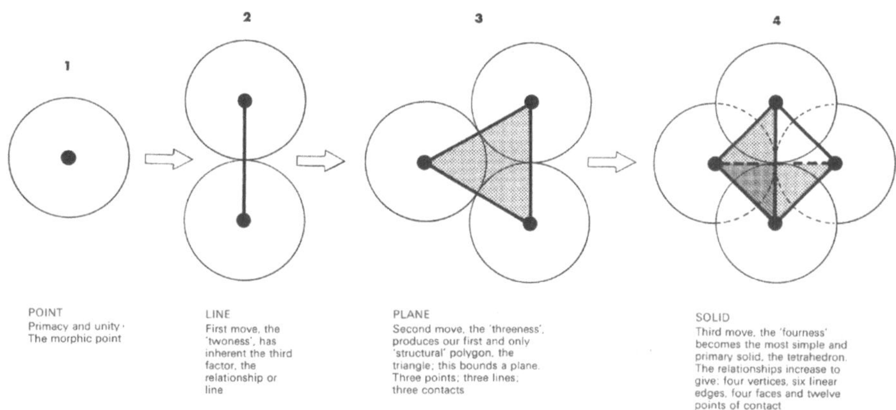

geometrical shapes by a.g. smith
order in space by peter critchlow

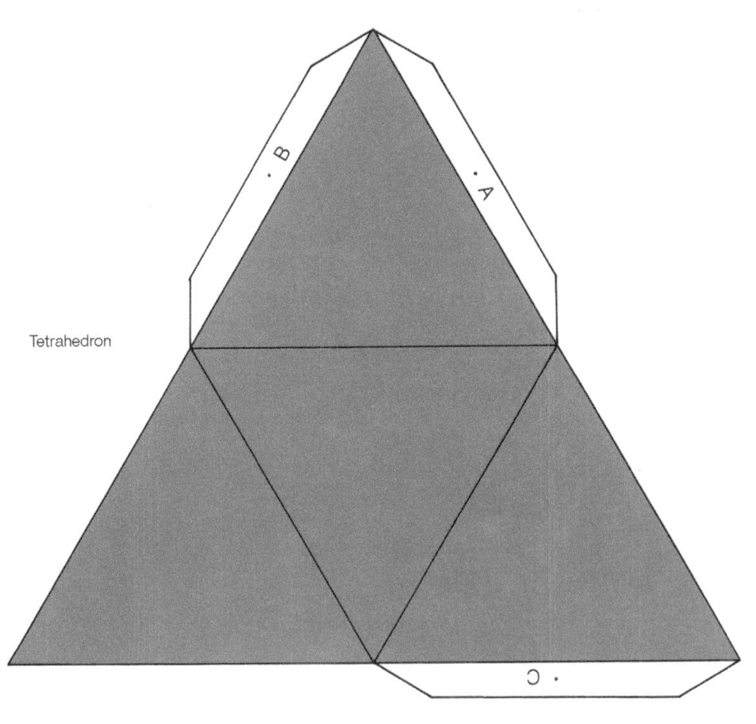

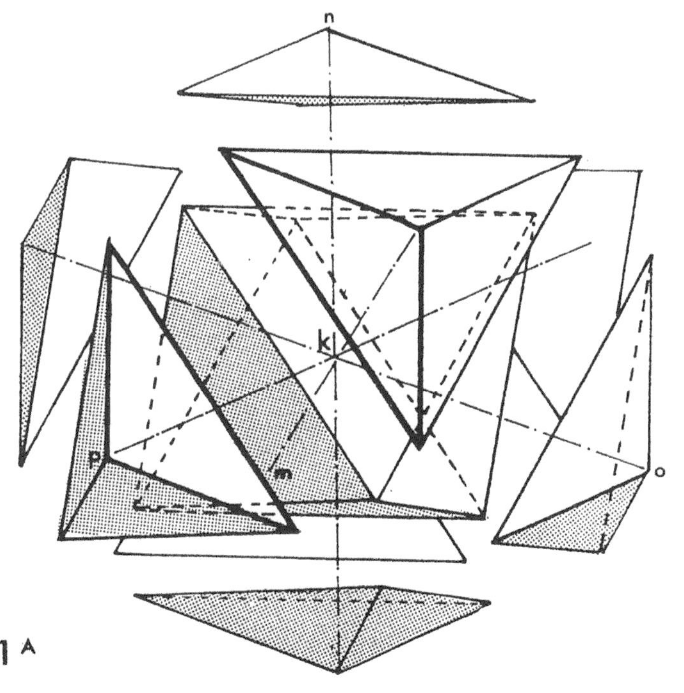

1 A

AS THIS, SO THAT

learning to listen, to see, and to form

Song of the Birds

Victor Hugo

Life! Oh joy! Deep woods,
We are alive.
Endless flight entreats us;
Let us float upon the air,
o'er the waters!
Birds
Are made of soul-dust.

Come soar! Fly
To the vales,
To the grottos, the shade,
　　　the places of respite!
Let us loose ourselves in this
Eternal sea
Where the cloud is an island!

From the heart of
　　　rocks and rushes,
From turrets,
From mounts which
　　　day sets ablaze,
Let us fly,
　　　and, quivering, mad,
Plunge
Into indescribable ecstasy!

Fly, birds, to the bell towers,
To the promontories,
To the cliffs,
　　　the mountain peaks,
To the glaciers, lakes
　　　and meadows;
Savor
Your freedom from the abyss!

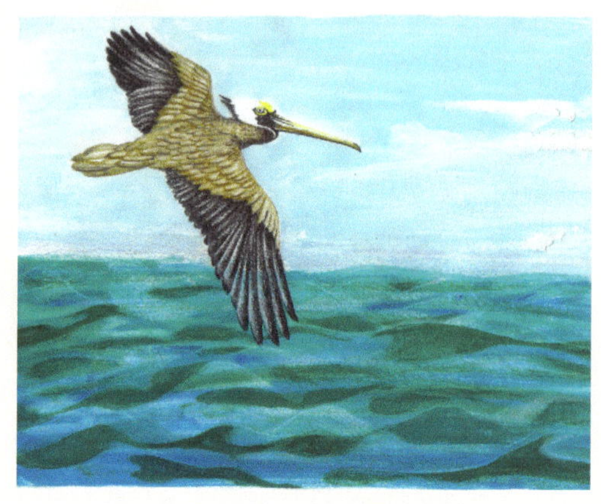

Conference of Birds

HOPE, rather resolutely, addressed the conference and proclaimed " Birds, you must now mediate your claim to the space between heaven and this domain.

You must determine how to imitate a cloud … and carve out space in its ethe-real-shroud?"

HOPE urged the primacy of Geometries incontrovertible TRUTH in its spacial determination. "Geometry is Natural! It is a Tool and not a style of choice! It is a rewarding tool of utilitarian language for the confabulation of space and form. It is a tried and true path to knowledge. Its exclusion in favoring phantasmagoric-res-olutions tends to leave behind universal reliability of basic logic when forming unity in purpose and action."

HOPE, whispered to the Birds calmly, "What is important in all this is HAV-

ING knowledge, not just having a theory about what may be known. To accept that there is a difference between faithful demonstration and the imprecision of persuasion.

PERSUASION countered, urging the Birds to include consideration of the probable and plausible; … the what-if's, "Must we be required to resort only to the proof texts of Geometry? Is there no possibility of resolution by way of NATURAL, spontaneous expression of the artisan?"

HOPE interrupted brashly, "Geom-etry' is NATURAL! Was the wheel invented so that each new genera-tion would drag it across the room? 'Geometry' is NATURAL!"

PERSUASION nodded in agreement, reinforcing Hope's initiative for the primacy of geometries tools, but begging inclusion in conceding that perhaps both must be considered.

"What is so feared", HOPE asked, "in folding a geometric shape? Is it the complicated names of their forms, like the names of dinosaurs? Is it the mysterious spaces and angular dimensions that lay hidden within them?"

PERSUASION reminded the Birds that three dimensional form was also feared in Flatland [1884]… "so feared that they were prohibited. Their mere mention was punishable by death." [Flatland, Abbott] The fiction of the place called Flatland underscored the limitations perpet-uated by an enduring metaphor that played on the Fear of Geometry, on the Fear and acknowledgment of Multiple Dimensions of form … or thought.

End of Episode Eight

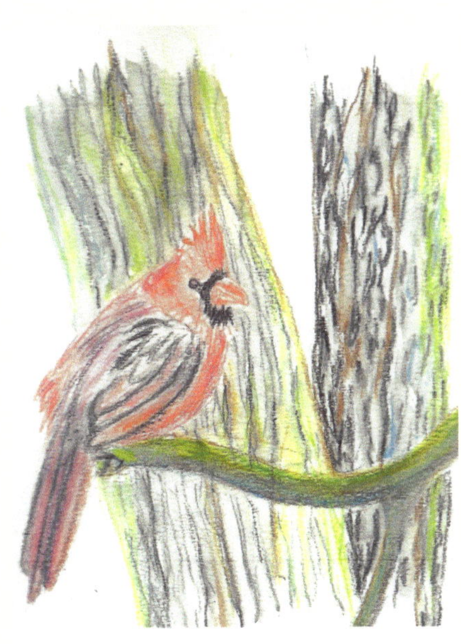

Assignment Ten:

To quell those fears Owl recommended A Mollification or Modification of inquiry, here-to-fore, issued and encouraged by HOPE and PERSUASION:

1] Participants were to Fold the attached geometric Template. Fold them in whatever manner, to create a nested shelter for the Bird and its Chicks.

2] Manipulate the Templates as you would a sketch or analysis … cut away, fold back, twist or curl the planes, or even shred its parts … to allow a nest to emerge as an interior space within an outer shell!

3] Cut and Fold the Template differently at least three times.

4] Choose to experiment with its planes using other medium like clay, glass, metal, or materials found in Natures landscape using the Template format.

5] Draw the most satisfactory resulting configuration. Articulate shade, shadow and light as you would a compositional still life. 'Likely' residents may be included in the Drawings.

"Now keep in mind", introjected OWL, "that in BIRD space 'stability' is dependent on [pyramidical] triangulation, like a truss or woven mesh. There need be no floor, no horizontal datum on which to walk, no planar roof to drain or grounding of its material to the earth. The Pyramid is an independent continuum of four its planes. Its Multiple surfaces [or faces] can facilitate an external and internal niche."

"It is about the forming of a concept of 'space' not 'a shape', … which will lead to and originate form. As a concept of space, and not of shape, … it will lead to the generation of its function. The tool of 'Geometry' is not only utilized to fulfill spatial function or whimsical fiction … but also to remind humankind, through its symbolic aspect, of the spiritual principles of an inner being.

HAVE FUN AND KEEP SMILING!

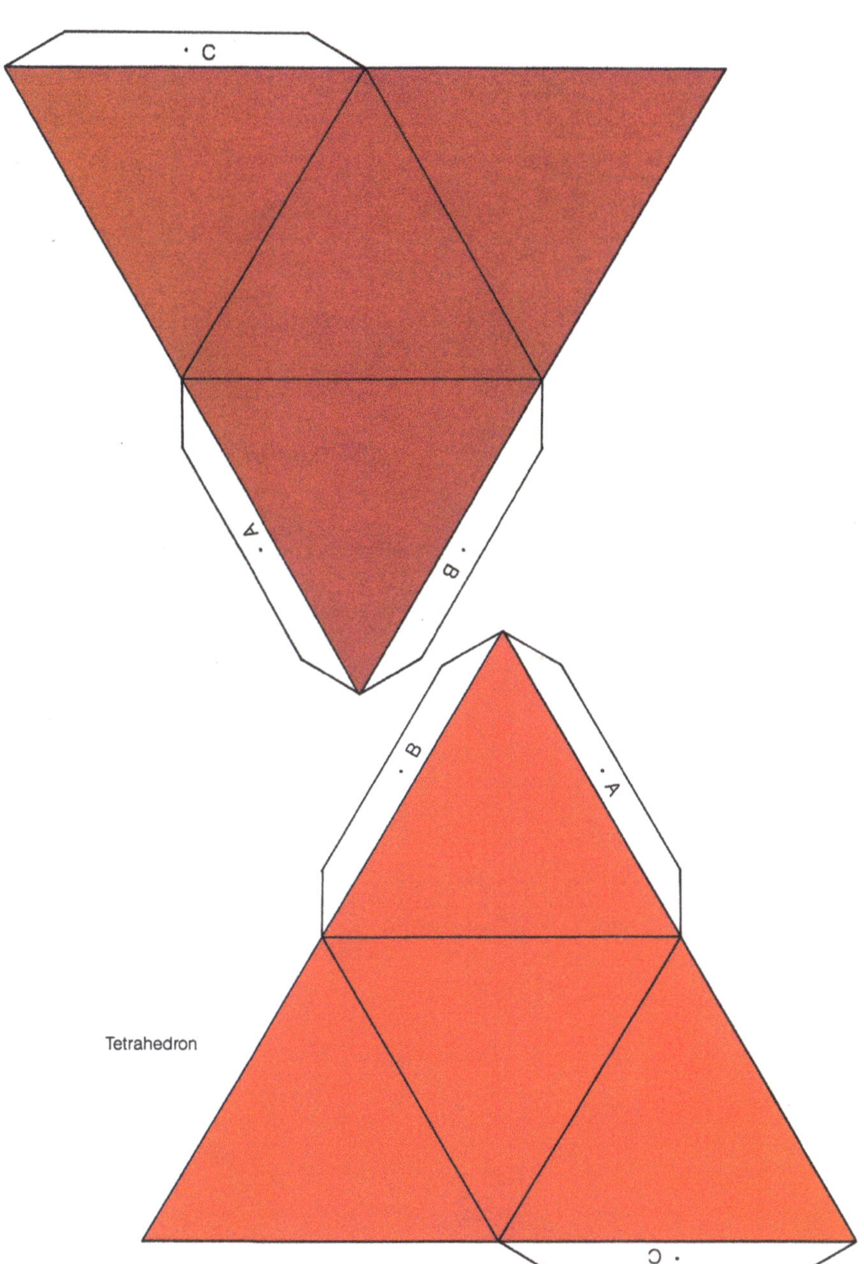

Tetrahedron

AS THIS, SO THAT

learning to listen, to see, and to form

Burnt Norton I

t.s.eliot

Time present and time past
Are both perhaps present in time future,
And time future contained in time past.
If all time is eternally present
All time is unredeemable.
What might have been is an abstraction
Remaining a perpetual possibility
Only in a world of speculation.
What might have been and what has been
Point to one end, which is always present.
Footfalls echo in the memory
Down the passage which we did not take
Towards the door we never opened
Into the rose-garden. My words echo
Thus, in your mind.
       But to what purpose
Disturbing the dust on a bowl of rose-leaves
I do not know.
       Other echoes
Inhabit the garden. Shall we follow?
Quick, said the bird, find them, find them,
Round the corner. Through the first gate,
Into our first world, shall we follow
The deception of the thrush?Into our first world.
There they were, dignified, invisible,
Moving without pressure, over dead leaves,

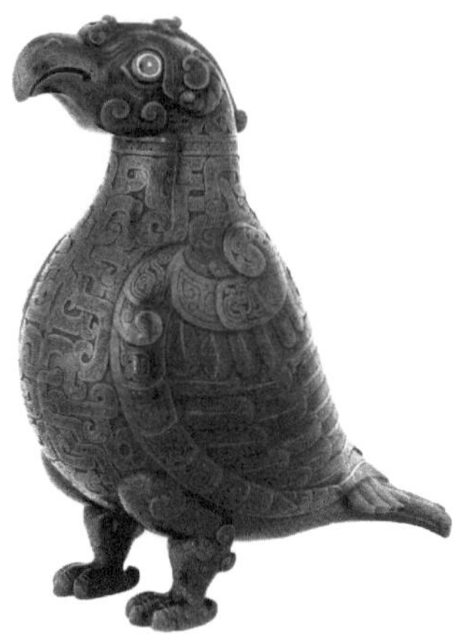

Conference of Birds

"Then," HOPE, PERSUASION and I "sat silent on top of the world. We saw below our feet, forests, cities, castles and a range of summits ...... We sat in silent contemplation of what was known, what forgotten, and what possible for our Cityscape … in theory and method.":

The object of eloquence is persuasion, the object of history is instruction, the object of poetry is to please by means of imagination and the passions, and the object of speculation is aspiration in bridging the yawning

In the autumn heat, through the vibrant air,
And the bird called, in response to
The unheard music hidden in the shrubbery,
And the unseen eye-beam crossed, for the roses
Had the look of flowers that are looked at.
There they were as our guests,
accepted and accepting.
So we moved, and they, in a formal pattern,
Along the empty alley, into the box circle,
To look down into the drained pool.
Dry the pool, dry concrete, brown edged,
And the pool was filled
with water out of sunlight,
And the lotos rose, quietly, quietly,
The surface glittered out of heart of light,
And they were behind us,
reflected in the pool.
Then a cloud passed,
and the pool was empty.
Go, said the bird, for the leaves were full
of children,
Hidden excitedly, containing laughter.
Go, go, go, said the bird: human kind
Cannot bear very much reality.
Time past and time future
What might have been
and what has been
Point to one end,
which is always present.

gulf between reality, set on the footing of the past, and its promise of untethered futurity.

PERSUASION'S, object was eloquence; HOPE'S, object was Instruction; and I, as SPECULATION, had as object the aspiration of bridging that yawning gulf between reality and futurity. In gnostic concordance, we sat silent on top of the world to espy its prosaic voice.

We noted the absence of classical other-worlds or underworlds. Their unseen populations of imagined angels and incorporeal messengers had been banished from illusory sight. The stars, rendered nameless, no longer displayed signs to serve as measurers or presenters of infinite abstracted thought. No longer read, their epical visions lost their application in ordering navigation or soothsaying. The sky's illiterate emptiness, being intolerable to humankind, prompted a spontaneous generation of new populations of protectors, messengers and seers to fill the apparent void.

Out of an anonymous psyche, humanity endeavored to fashion corporeal images to fill or fulfill the caverness void.

The resulting handiwork did not resemble the graceful angels, faeries or mystical guides they had known in prior existences. The brightly colored distinguishing feathers offering attributes of enlightened comfort were errant in the disposition of invention. Demonic and devouring monsters, aliens and miscreants recognizably tied to the absence of parentage or mythical metamorphosis, un-entombed themselves, teeming upward towards infinities universe. Representative of nightmares in lieu of dreams and of fear in lieu of aspirations they effaced the trace of the planetary orbits.

Desires necessity of looking skyward was denigrated as these transitory imaginings were projected and electronically imposed on cinematic Silver-Screens. Daily folded-papers awarded them 'Oscars'; shiny gilded miniature idols reminiscent of images from the kilns of Canaan. The 'allure' of these Awards further inspired the invention of droids, satanic war mongers, probes, action figures, plastic nodding bobble headed Heroes, Frankensteins, werewolves [in homage to the full moon], and even flying Spiders. Iconic replicas of these newly fashioned figures were made readily available for purchase at FAO Schwartz … no longer necessitating pilgrimage to heavenly Temples.

These misshapen dysmorphic beings' presence diminished predictably as expected for all short lived NEW commodities. No longer meriting commercial benefit, they metamorphosed into the category of Nostalgia and then vanished. A vague appearance of the 'disappeared' clutched at the shadows of the soothsayer Generals and CEOs.

The sky, in its exhausted emptiness, emitted overtones and prophetic warnings of the advent of an approaching doomsday; an apocalyptic event of unmitigated erasure.

HOPE, PERSUASION and SPECULATION theretofore approved the proposed rational for the immediate Exodus and the Construction of their alternative city … as mandatory.

[Volume 2 11/18/2020]

Yet always there is another life,
A life beyond this present knowing,
A life brighter than this present splendor,
Brighter, perfected and distant away,
Not to be reached but to be known,
Not an attainment of the will
But something illogically received,
A divination, a letting down
From loftiness, misgivings dazzlingly
Resolved in dazzling discovery.

Wallace Stevens. [1879-1955]

"Go, go, go, said the bird:
human kind
Cannot bear very much more
reality …"

t.s.eliot

Now, we return to PERSUASION'S proposal for the new City between the Earth and the Sky. A City-In-the-Air to hold the heavens in place above the earth. "Imagine," PERSUASION pled, "a City in the Air, between the below and the above, and not devoid of the implications of referent-knowledge. In the Air and above the Horizon, and not sup-planted by the vertical Silver-Screen.

[Volume 2 11/18/20]

HOPE a geometer, measured the air geometrically in proportion to the earth.

Alighting 'with a piece of string, a straight edge and a shadow, the Bird's embarked on charting Forms and Foundations for the proposed aerial cityscape.

Fabricating simple forms, as cut-outs and fold-ups, they relied upon the gravitation-less sky and securely in-serted independent stable geomet-ric forms. The Pyramid [tetrahedron] their first challenge, was inspired by the mystical theories of the Egyp-tians, Freemasons and Ben Franklin's design of the dollar bill.

Re-discovering the mysterious stability of the tetrahedron they constructed their first nested-neigh-borhood-complex.

"Now" this concludes the ninth volume of our newsletter. In order to commit to completing this first chap-ter of our venture, it is requested that all participants and recipients of this RAG submit a drawing, model, poem, fable, editorial or whatever, to assist in a conclusory TENTH VOL-UME EDITION so that we may alight upon the Construction Phase of the City CQ with assured determination.

Please send your contribution for the TENTH VOLUME of this news-letter by e-mail or via carrier-pigeon … to our bird-house-box … Thank-ing you in advance.

Editor in residence,
SPECULATION, v.r.w.

End of Episode Nine

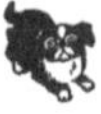

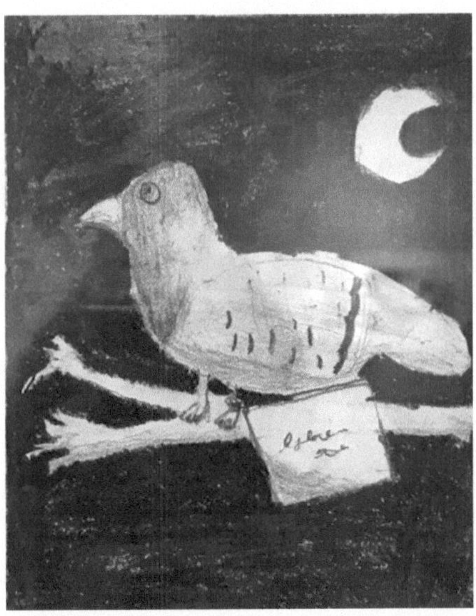

Assignment Eleven:
Tetrahedron

Fold some tetrahedrons for a proposed multiple-family-bird-complex.

See Volume 8 for templates.

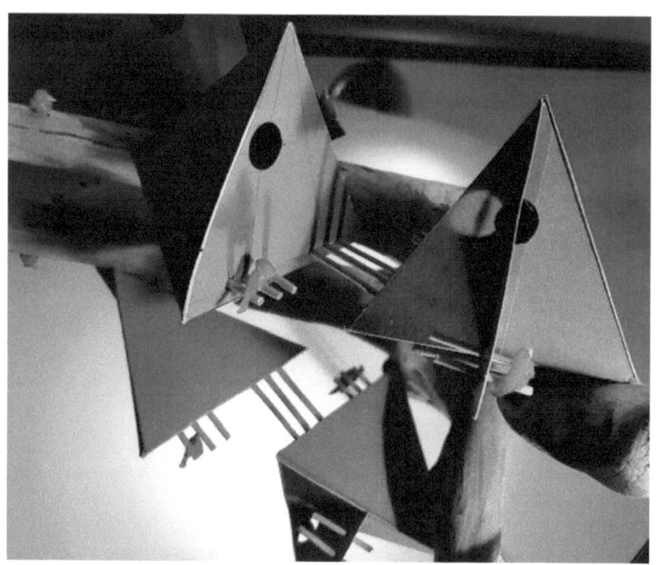

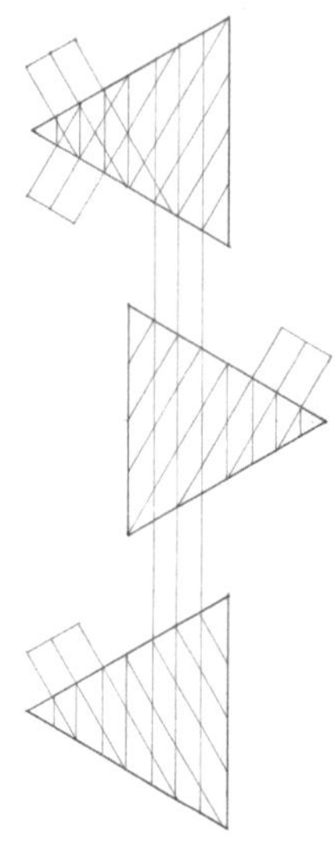

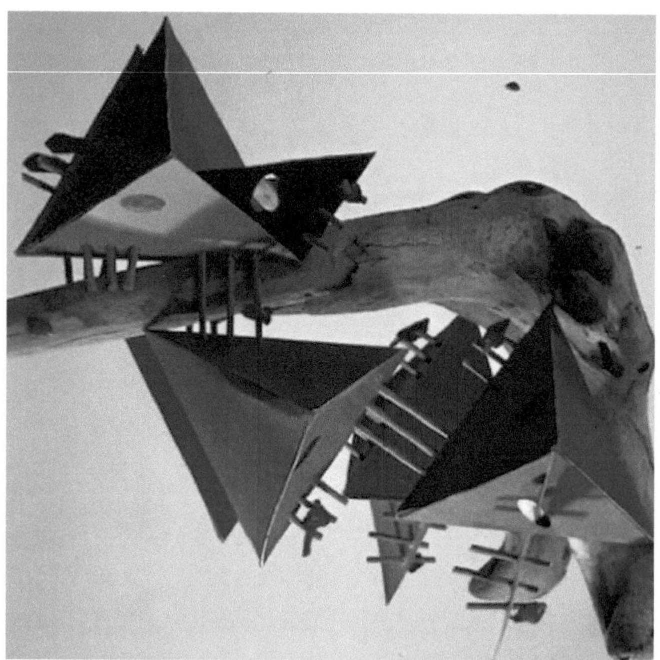

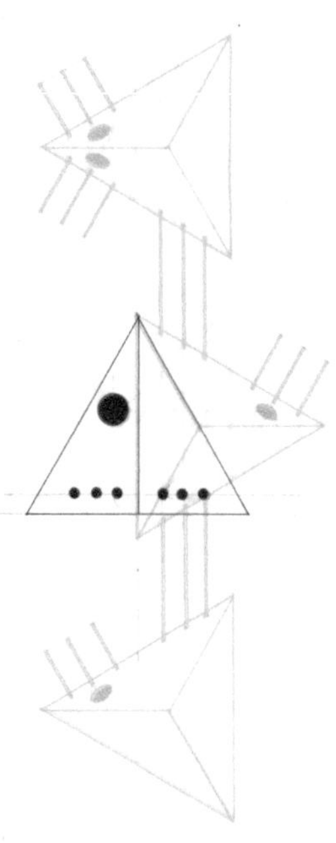

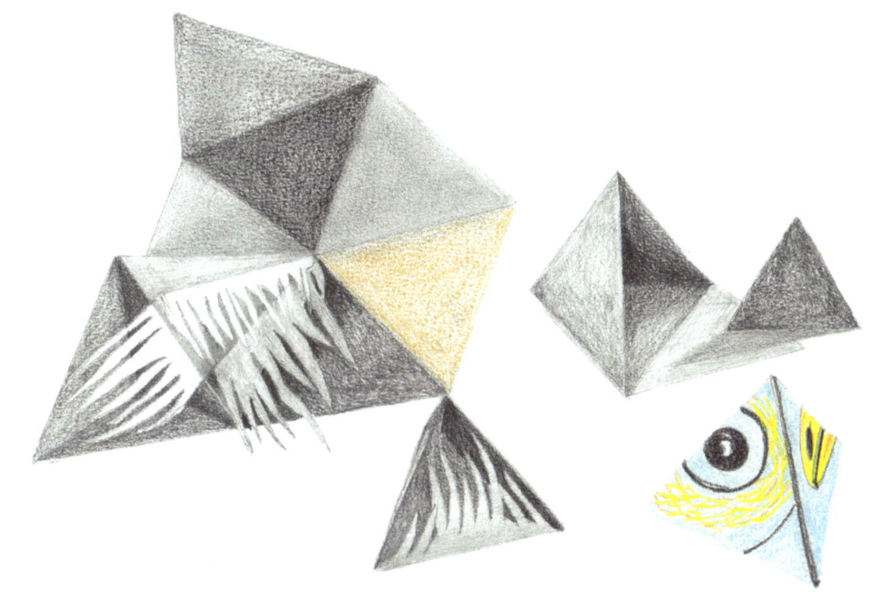

Partita on a Tetrahedron

"It is not everyday that the world arranges itself in a poem"

w.stevens

The **TETRAHEDRON** has four equal sides. The number FOUR is connected to the first known ordering number in the world and points to the change from nature to civilization.

The **CUBE** has SIX equal sides all meeting at perpendicular angles. It is the ideal form for any closed construction. SIX is the first perfect number … having the sum and product of its parts being equal. The world was created/perfected in SIX days; on its first day Light was created, on the second and third days Heaven and Earth were created, and on the last three days were created individual Creatures from fish to birds to humans.

CUT, FOLD and DRAW the CUBE.

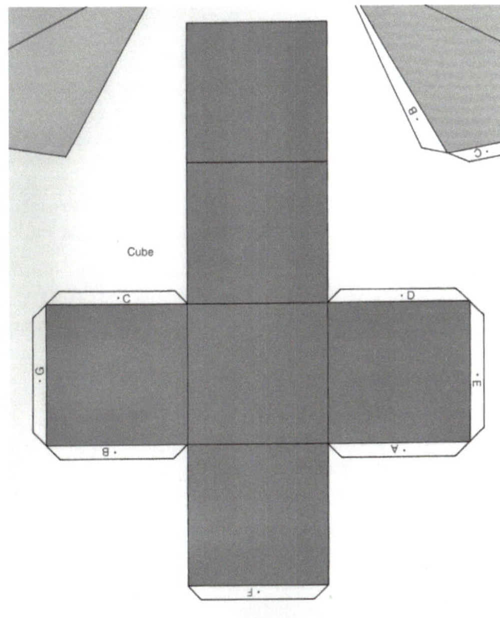

AS THIS, SO THAT
learning to listen, to see, and to focus

the Dream

Maulana Jalaluddin Rumi
Oh, if a tree could wander
and move with foot and wings!
It would not suffer the ax blows
nor feel pain of saws!
For if the sun did not wander
away in every night —
How could at ev'ry morning
the world be lighted up?
And if the ocean's water
did not rise to the sky,
How would the plants be quickened
by streams and gentle rain?
The drop that left its homeland,
the sea, and then returned —
It found an oyster waiting
and grew into a pearl.
Did Yusuf not leave his father,
in grief, tears and despair?
Did he not, by such a journey,
gain kingdom and fortune wide?
Did he not the prophet travel
to far Medina, friend?
And there he found a new kingdom
and ruled a hundred lands.
You lack a foot to travel?
Then journey into yourself,
And like a mine of rubies
receive the sunbeams' print!
Out of yourself — such a journey
will lead you to your self,
It leads to transformation
of dust into pure gold!
Leave bitterness and acid,
go forth to sweetness now!
For even brine produces
a thousand kinds of fruits.
It is the Sun of Tabriz
that does such wondrous work,
For every tree gains beauty,
when touched by the sun.

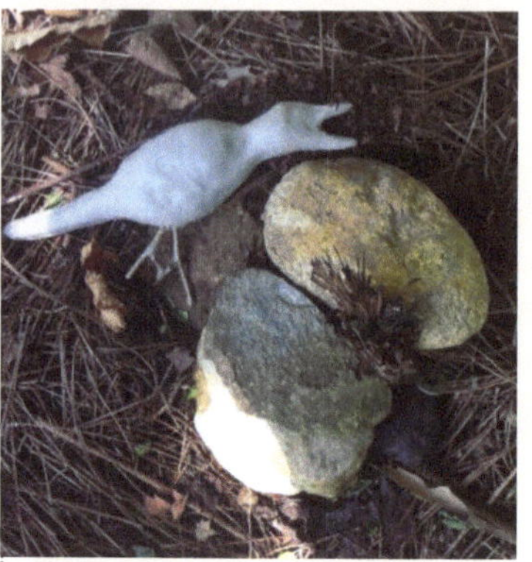

Conference of Birds

"This bird came to me in a dream, the moving beak crying for the world in grief. It had been placed on my cat Pogo's grave last summer. Its clay has by now dissolved back into the earth. It had been made of purge clay with just that intent … to return to the earth, carrying grief and mourning with it. It seemed as if it was a form of navigation for the spirit.".

Maria Epes

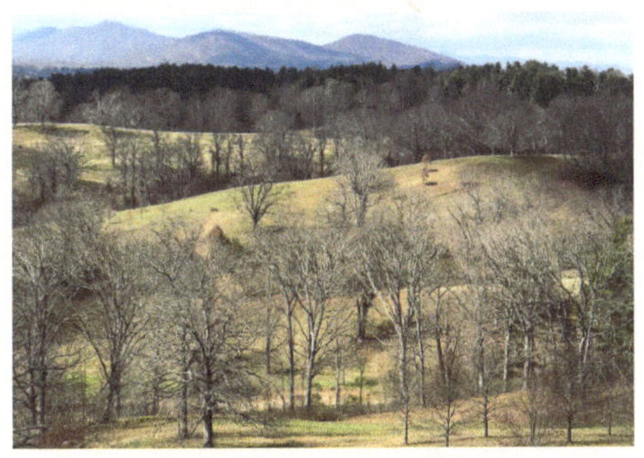

The belief that animals in general and birds in particular convey messages, omens and signs appear in all ancient sources. Ornithomancy is not explicitly mentioned, however it has diverse representation in literature including quoted texts by those of greater Wisdom. For example, Solomon's conversations with birds does not perceive his conduct as a type of divination but rather presents it as a manifestation of his excessive Wisdom.

'In Solomon's dream the Creator of the World appeared and asked "what shall I give you?" Solomon remembers answering, "If I were to ask for silver, gold and jewels you would give them to me … but I ask only for Wisdom." After awakening it is said that Solomon was aware of understanding the languages of all the animals and well as the meaning of the birds chirping.'

A. Schimmel
I am The Wind, You are The Fire

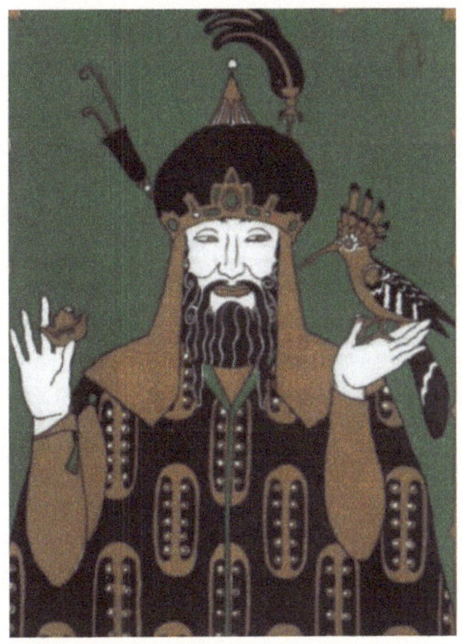

"It is more than just grief felt in passing from the 'Now 'towards the 'Thou'. More than grief, in its final exhalation, burdened by sentient memory. This clay Bird, in grief, passes through the diaphanous skin of the clay-world- Earth, passes through its cleansing sieve, to return to its forgotten first song of freedom."

Maria Epes

End of Episode Ten

Now we have completed another 'decade' or 'generation' of assignments, group studios and recorded works as Axiom Maxiom Participants. This completion defines the resilience of the heart's-soul as an ever replenishing self polishing mirror. Its radiant reflection of 'will' appeared in the mirror and became, as it were, a multiplicity of mirrors for each other … in a Community of creativity. I present at this time a literal cliff hanger for what will transpire next in our future studios. Commencing in the warmer spring weather of May … with new questions, materials and challenges, we can once again share this Axiom Maxiom experiment.

AS IF .... SO THEN

a journal of speculation

Hafiz: The Tree OF Life

Emerson, Persian Poetry

" My phoenix long ago secured
      His nest in the sky-vault's cope;
In the body's cage immured,
      He was weary of life's hope.

"Round and round his heap of ashes,
      Now flies the bird amain.
But in that odorous niche of heaven
      Nestles the bird again.

"Once flees he upward, he will perch
      On Tuba's* golden bough;
His home is on that fruited arch
      Which cools the blest below.

"If over this world of ours
      His wings my phoenix spread,
How gracious falls on land and sea
      The soul-refreshing shade!

"Either world inhabits he,
      Sees oft below him planets roll;
His body is all of air compact,
      Of Spirit's love his soul."

[*Tuba's bough=sacred tree of Paradise]

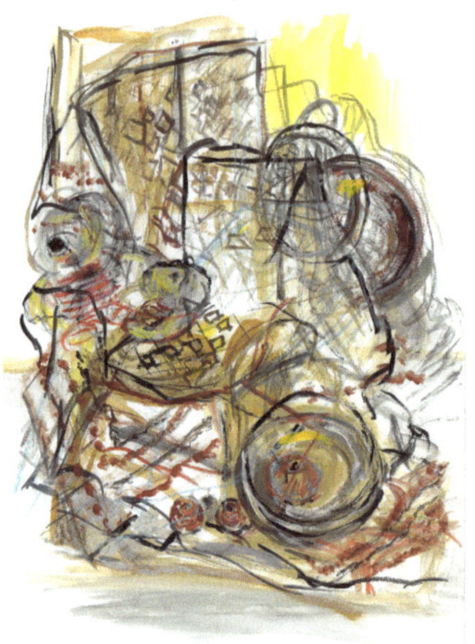

Timely Talisman

"… Solomon had three talisman: first, the signet-ring by which he commanded the spirits, on the stone of which was engraved the Name; second, the glass in which he saw the secrets of his enemies and the causes of all things; the third, the east wind, which was his horse.

His counsellor was Simorg, king of birds, the all wise fowl who had lived ever since the beginning of the world, and now lives alone on the highest summit of Mount Kaf. By him Solomon was taught the language of birds, so that he heard secrets whenever he went into his gardens.

When Solomon travelled, his throne
was placed on a carpet of green silk,
of a length and breadth sufficient for
all his army to stand upon, — men
placing themselves on his right hand,
and the spirits on his left. When all
were in order, the East Wind, at his
command, took up the carpet and
transported it with all that were
upon it, whither he pleased, — the
army of birds at the same time flying
overhead and forming a canopy to
shade them from the sun."

Emerson, Persian Poetry:
Excerpt on Solomon

…As accorded by Emerson, Solomon relied
on three prescribed talisman attributed to the
successful outcome of his undertakings.

Timely Talisman

What is a talisman? Why are there
three? How are they chosen? How
are they defined but not deified?

The use of talisman is world wide
among almost all peoples. It is familiar to all Americans in the form of
horseshoes, lucky coins or tee shirt, a
rabbits foot, mustard seeds or garlic.
They are, for some, considered won-
der working objects given the power
to secure good fortune and success
in ones undertakings. What three
talisman insures hopeful outcomes
for you?

"…then, in one moment, she put
forth the charm
with woven paces and waving
hands."

Tennyson, Vivien

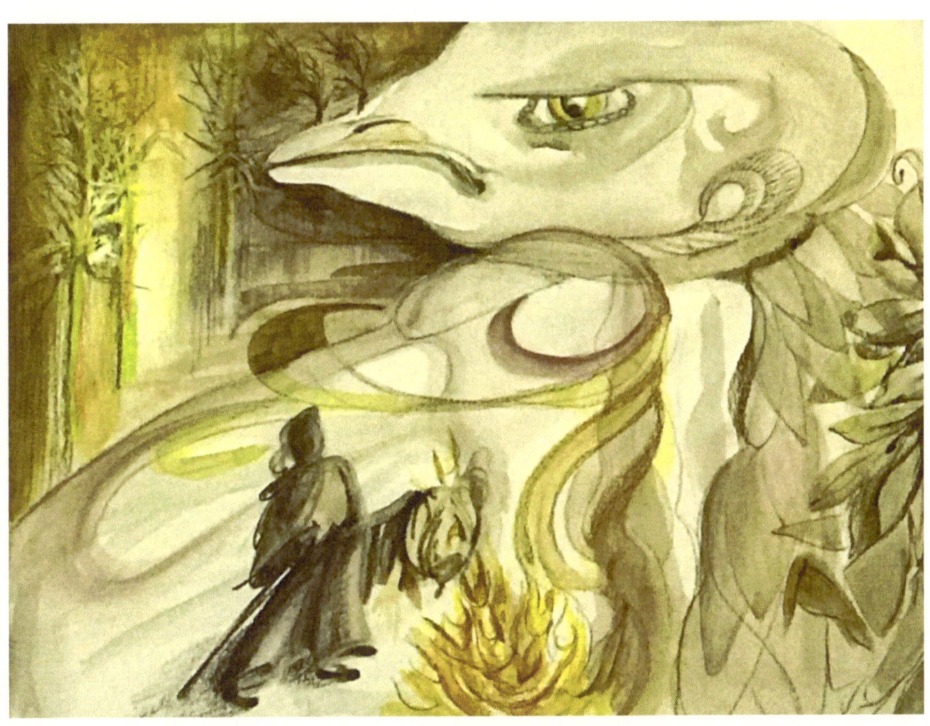

Assignment Twelve

Make three copies of the square-study Template on opaque paper [A,B,C] and one copy [D] on transparent paper.

Drawing A:
Draw your personal or imagined talisman be it a coin, a ring, a rabbits foot or lucky tee shirt. Draw it with perseverance and awe. Compose it in the square template accounting for its light, shadow and placement in space.

Drawing B:
The glass through which you see … is the language of your thinking and speech. Write a message, in mirror image, upon a reflective surface. [mirror, pond, ocean, etc.]. The message can be from or to a Bird in your garden. Draw its energy.

Drawing C:
Solomon relied on the power of the East Wind for energy … equally powerful would be gusts of spring color, the swift passage of time or your imaginative capacity to speculate. Draw the Power that compels your Bird to Draw or Paint the "Spring of a hopeful 2021".

Drawing D:
On the transparent template superimpose the above three drawings to form one composition. You can change the scale of any layer by enlarging or shrinking the images … the three images reveal your secret powers. Frame it with one of the six primary forms.

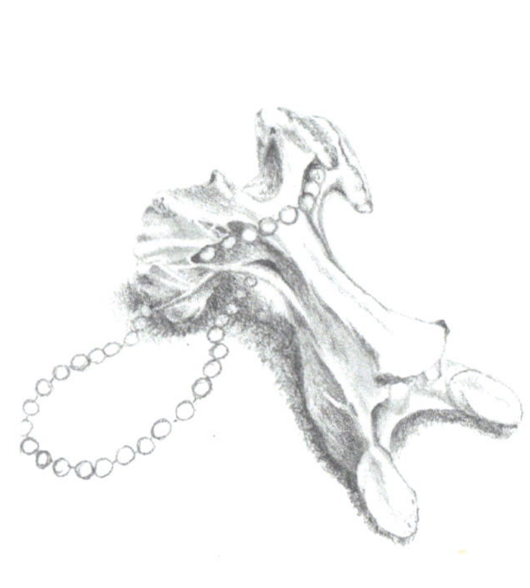

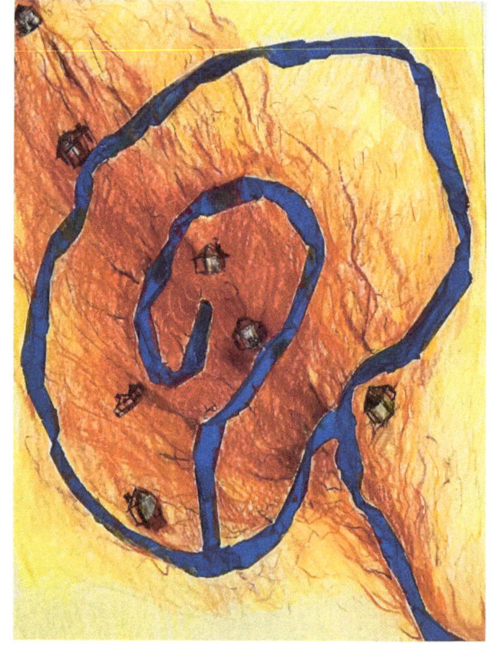

AS IF .... SO THEN

covid competition: from competer {Latin}
to strive for ... as a resolution

A request for submission of drawing, graphic or model to

address the current necessity of a 'STANDARD FORM' for documentation of Covid Vaccination and or Treatment.

Submission to include, but not limited to, Items #1through #9 below.

Submission due-date: May 3, 2021

---

1. passe' per tout:

-giving permission to travel everywhere [even in-time, via time capsule at no extra cost].

> *Password: shibboleth [watchword to distinguish ones own from others betrayed by the pronunciation sibboleth; [Judges xii.6]*

---

2. VACCINATION RECORD

LAST NAME:____

FIRST NAME: ____

DATE OF BIRTH: _________________________

1st Dose Covid-19: DATE: ____________ PRODUCT LOT#___________

2nd Dose Covis-19: DATE: ____________ PRODUCT LOT#___________

Other: DATE:______________________ PRODUCT LOT#___________

Other: DATE:______________________ PRODUCT LOT# __________

3. REACTIONS

ADVERSE REACTIONS:

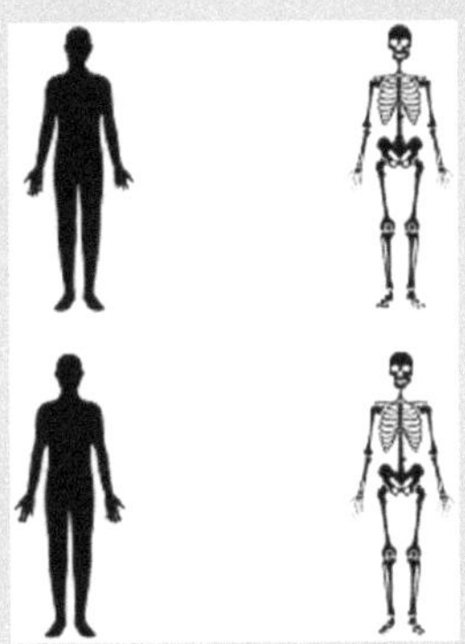

LINGERING EFFECTS:

---

4. DAILY OPTIMISM LEVEL

Scale A to Z

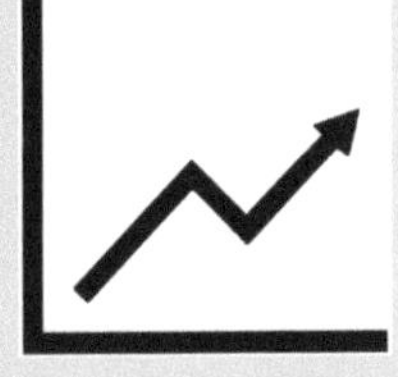

monday   tuesday   wednesday   thursday   friday   saturday   sunday

---

5. SELF PORTRAIT: BEFORE VACCINATION

6. SELF PORTRAIT: AFTER VACCINATION

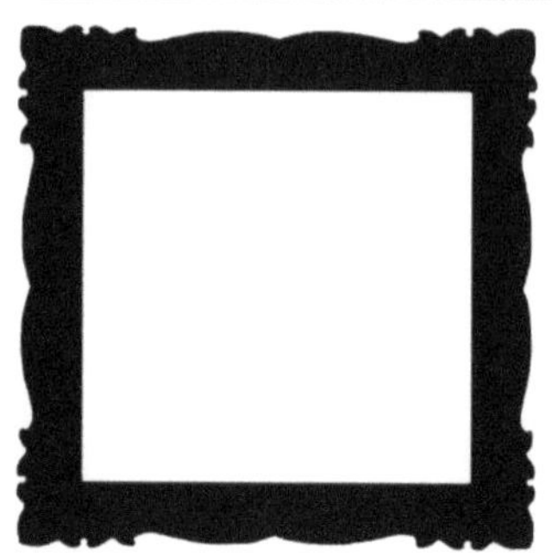

7. FUTUR-ITY PORTRAIT: SO THEN...................

8. DNA SAMPLE:

____

____

9. TIME CAPSULE:

Instructions:

Cut and fold a form or cube* according to its fold lines and tabs. Attach items #2 thru #7 to the exterior of the form. [see below for suggestion]. Insert your sample DNA, Item #8, [hair, nail, or other] into the form. Insert the form in a closed tube/capsule, Item #9 right. The capsule will be BURIED in a protected location for future Archeologist's Discovery in 3031 CE.

FORM

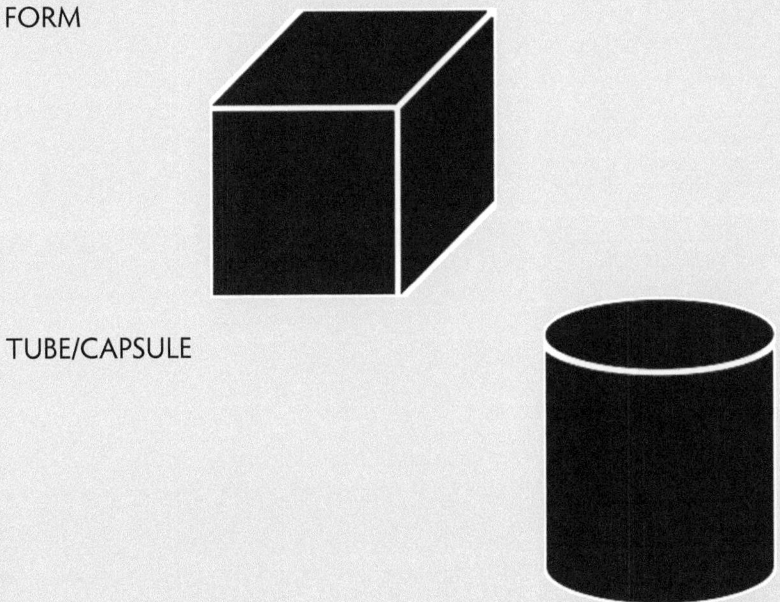

TUBE/CAPSULE

Send Submission to Axiom Maxiom: 5 Rollingwood Road, Asheville, NC 28805

Commendable Submissions to be installed at the Axiom Maxiom Gallery.
regiweile@axiom-maxiomdrawingcenter.com

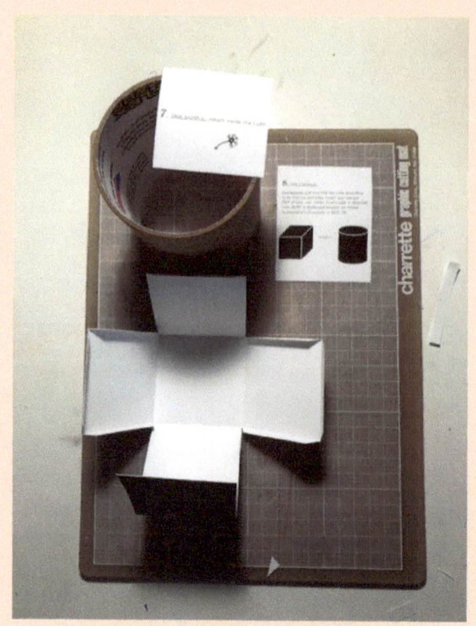
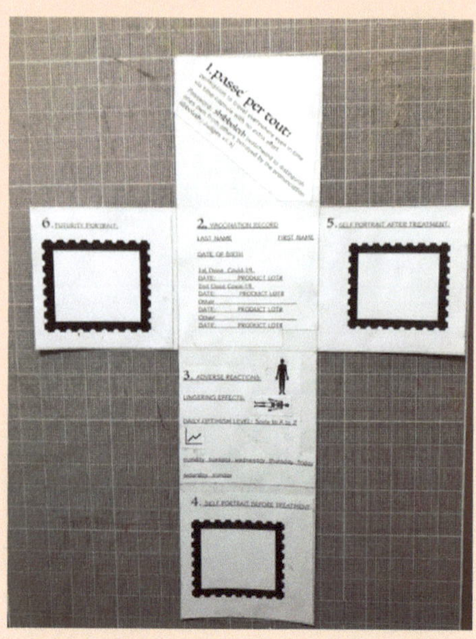
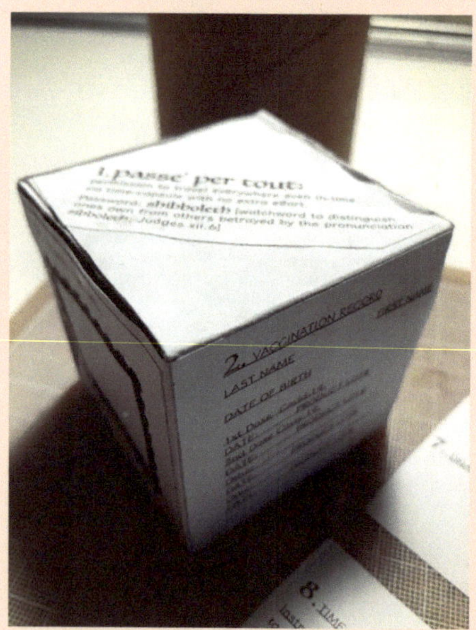
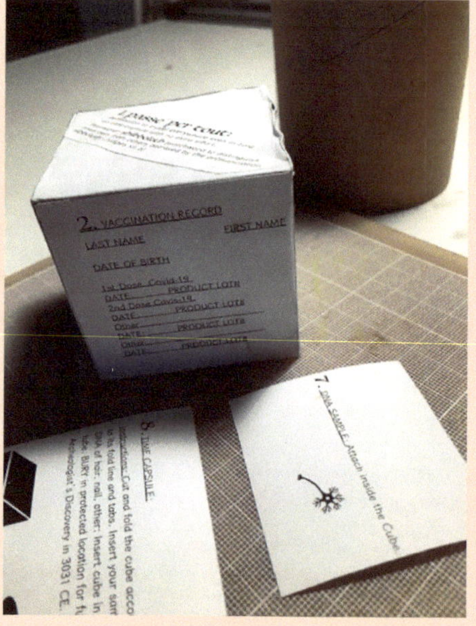

BIBLIOGRAPHICA

page	*citing*
pg. 6	Philo of Alexandria
pg. 8	Ralph Waldo Emerson; Birds
	Lewis Carroll; Quote
pg.12	Emily Dickinson; Birds 328
pg.13	Leonardo da Vinci; Quote
	Aristophanes Critique; Quote
pg.16	Aristophanes; the Clouds
pg. 22	Ben Sira; Search for Wisdom
pg. 25	Favid ud din Attar; Conference of Birds
pg. 28	Robert Browning; Abt Volger IV
	A.E. Abbott; Flatland Quote
pg. 30-31	Favid ud din Attar; a retelling of Conference of Birds
pg. 34	E.A. Abbott; Flatland Dedicatory
	Julia Diggens; Quote
pg. 38	A.G. Smith; Order in Space
pg. 40	Victor Hugo; Song of the Birds
pg. 44	TS Eliot; Burnt Norton I
pg. 46	Wallace Stevens; Quote
	TS Eliot; Burnt Norton I
pg. 49	Wallace Stevens; Quote
pg. 50	Maulana Jalaluddin Rumi; The Dream
pg. 50-51	Maria Epes; Quote
pg. 51	A. Shimmel; I am the Wind You Are the Fire
pg. 52	Ralph Waldo Emerson; Persian Poetry
pg. 53	Alfred Lord Tennyson; Vivian

PARTICIPANTS AND CONTRIBUTORS OF IMAGES

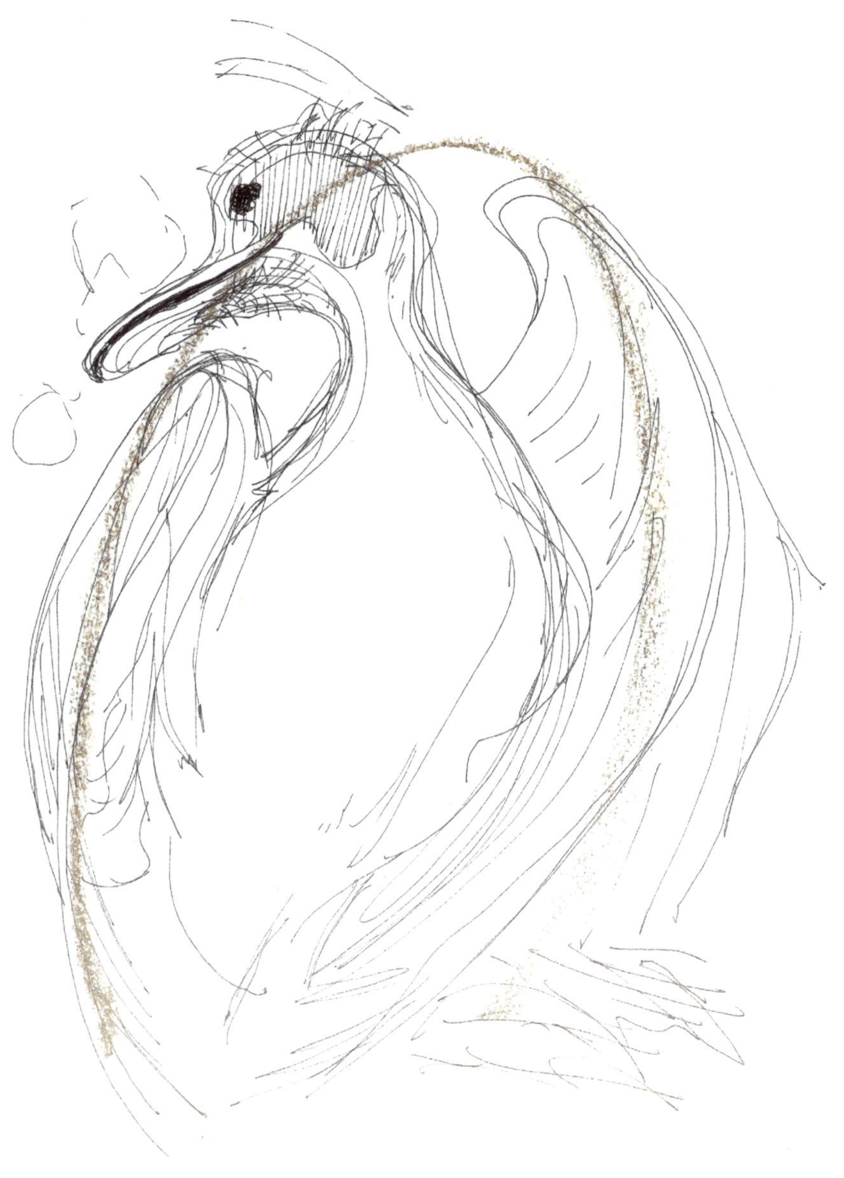